Growing Up Broken

Michelle White

This book is dedicated to all
the Marley's of the world

www.michellewhite.biz

Chapter 1: Early Years

October 1989

Most of the children have been picked up by their parents after the school Halloween party, but where are my mummy and daddy?

Mummy must be busy with my two-year-old sister, Charlotte and my month-old brother, Toby. But what about my daddy? I'm guessing he has already started drinking. Daddy is always drinking and he's always getting really angry with me.

I know they've forgotten that I'm here but if the school phone them, it will be my fault, I'll be the one in trouble and I really don't want that. I notice the teachers are talking to some of the other parents and spot this as the opportunity to slip away without anybody noticing. That's exactly what I did.

It's a very cold and particularly dark evening. We live on the north coast of Scotland in Aberdeenshire, in a small, but fairly busy, fishing town. The air here is so very fresh. There is almost always a strong gustily breeze coming in from the seafront. All you can hear around town are the big North Sea waves crashing against the sea wall. I do love the sound of the waves.

The seafront doesn't have any sand, instead it's a coastline full of stones, you can't even walk barefoot on them because it really hurts your feet. I would love to one day walk on a nice sandy beach; don't you think that would be lovely? There are lots of fishing boats, all different shapes and sizes, they are all very noisy indeed, I hear them all through the night sounding off their fog horns. Sometimes when I hear them, I'll make the same noise just to make my little sister laugh, she is so cute when she is giggling.

I am freezing cold. All I am wearing is my underwear and a black bin bag, with holes cut out for my arms. I didn't have a costume to wear so my parents put this on me and they told me to say I had come as a witch. They had tied a piece of string around the waist to shape it up a bit.

My name is Marley and I'm five years old. I have very pale Scottish skin with lots of freckles across my nose and really big blue eyes. My hair is dark brown and very thick, it is broken in many places and I have lots of short bits. I hate having my hair brushed because it hurts so much, there must be a way to brush hair without it hurting.

I walk a little over half a mile to school every day with my older brother, Tom. I'm used to walking the same route everyday but I'm never usually on my own, I really don't like this feeling of walking on my own now. I'm starting to feel quite nervous and a little bit scared. There are a lot of people out, all wearing their Halloween costumes, some of them look incredibly scary. If I don't look anyone in the eye and just focus on making my way home, then I guess all will be well.

I am getting closer to home now but as I approach my house, I start to get a nervous feeling inside of my belly and my mind is telling me that I'm going to be in trouble.

Although those feelings grow with intensity the closer to home I get, I am feeling a slight sense of relief that I have made it here safely. I pluck up the courage to knock on the door, but no one answers. Maybe I didn't knock hard enough. So, I knock again but this time I knock much harder. A few moments later I see the light come on through the glass of the front door and the silhouette of my daddy coming towards it. He opens the door and look's down at me with a confused look on his face, the confusion quickly changes to anger. I look up at my daddy and sheepishly say "you forgot to pick me up daddy and I didn't want you or mummy to get into any trouble, so I came home all by myself, that's good isn't it?". "You really are a stupid little girl Marley!! Get up those stairs and don't come down!!". I knew what was coming. As I ran through the door towards the stairs directly in front of me, I felt a hard slap on the back of my head.

I had felt that same smack so many times before. The sudden jolt hurt my neck every time it happened.

The thing is, they had forgotten me. It didn't matter what I did, either way I would have been in trouble. It seemed like everything I did, had some negative repercussion.

We lived on the main road in a house with a shop attached to the side of it. It always felt to me that it was a very old building. My parents had started a travel agency business from the shop. It was, to begin with, growing to become a pretty successful business. Work took up a lot of my parents focus and time, although it was good that they were effectively working from home.

The kitchen was at the back of the house, to the right of it was the door that led to an industrial looking utility room, in which was the doorway to the back of the shop. That meant that even if mummy and daddy were working, we knew where they were if we needed them.

Daddy had planned a trip to Kissimmee in Orlando, Florida. He was leaving mummy to manage the business and look after the children although he had booked my older brother, Tom, to go with him. I'm guessing that was to take some of the strain from mummy, or maybe it was just because he did not want to go alone.

The aim of the trip was to purchase a holiday home which they could hire out to holiday makers. I did wonder why he only chose to take Tom with him. I would have been really good if he'd taken me, I promised I wouldn't have been any trouble. I always tried so hard to be good. Thinking about it more, why were we all not going and making a holiday from it? Mummy really needed a break. They had staff employed who were experienced enough to run the shop in their absence. I still don't know or understand why he only chose to take Tom, it seemed really unfair.

I was very disappointed that I didn't get to go. I'd spent ages looking at brochures of Florida in my parents shop. I knew what was there and what an amazing place it would be to go.

I loved the thought of travelling the world and would dream of going on amazing family holidays. I decided if I ever had children when I was older, I wouldn't single mine out like that, I would take all my children to Florida.

Daddy and Tom went on the trip and they did all sorts of fun things whilst they were there. Daddy did end up buying a house too, but straight away it didn't go as well as they had planned. The house was broken into several times and it ended up being very costly.

Mummy was constantly stressed and looking exhausted. She was raising four children and trying to run the business. She was living six hundred miles away from her own family who lived in the East Anglia region in England. My daddy's family lived two hundred miles away in the southern part of Scotland. It all seemed very isolating. My parents didn't really have any friends or any form of a social life, well daddy kind of did, we lived opposite a pub and he spent a whole lot of time in there.

On very few occasions, my nanna & grandad would make the drive from Southern England to Northern Scotland to visit us, but we didn't see them often at all. It was a very long drive for them.

There was always a sense of disapproval and tension in the air when they were with us, I really don't think they liked daddy. However, I loved it when they made the effort to come and stay with us. I felt so safe and loved by my nanna. She gave me the warmest hugs and I know she knew that I wasn't a happy child. I used to cry so much when they had to go home again and leave me. I would watch their car drive away until they couldn't be seen anymore.

Following their departure would always come feelings of being scared and insecure. Those feelings would hit me like the waves hitting the sea wall and remain as an almost permanent state of mind.

I say almost because if I was on my own in my bedroom when I felt sad, I would try my hardest to block those negative thoughts out. I would try and think about nice things instead.

I would daydream, picturing myself with a life of bliss, the most perfect happy, loving mummy and daddy, eating a family picnic whilst myself and my siblings were running through green fields full of flowers, or playing with a swing tied to a branch on a tree. Visualisation was to become a friend of mine, it would be my coping mechanism.

The house we lived in needed a lot of work doing to it. It hadn't had any maintenance inside for a very long time and it was in desperate need of updating. My parents were trying to make the house more habitable and a much nicer place for us to live. There were only two rooms upstairs which were both bedrooms. At the top of the stairs to the left was my bedroom.

I was six years old when I got my own room. They decorated the walls in a baby pink colour with care bear wallpaper on one wall and a soft pink carpet. I felt so lucky and grateful that they had done it for me. There was an old fireplace with a brass fire guard which mummy and daddy bought especially for that fireplace. To each side of the fireplace were two built in cupboards with key and lock doors. The cupboard to the left had shelving and the cupboard to the right had a rail for clothes, it was so tall inside a grown up could easily stand up straight in it. I would often hear scratching noises from inside the cupboards at night. There were mice living in the cavities of the walls, the carpet which was laid in there was shredded as the mice would constantly chew on it. We had mouse traps set in the kitchen and quite often we'd be met in the morning with a mouse in a trap. I didn't like the mice at all.

My elder brother Tom had the other upstairs room, his was decorated in a baby blue colour with Thomas the tank engine wallpaper on one wall and a lovely soft pale blue carpet. His room didn't have cupboards or a fireplace like mine. Quite often my brother Tom would come into my room and play.

There was one particular and very unforgettable day when Tom came into my room. We were playing really quite roughly and he knocked me flying towards the fire guard, I fell on to it. My fall bent the fire guard. I tried to straighten it out but I couldn't get it back to how it was before, there was a kink in it which just wouldn't come out. I tried my best to straighten it before we carried on playing and I thought nothing more of it.

Later that day, I heard heavy footsteps coming up the stairs and knowing I'd damaged something, an instant feeling of dread appeared. My bedroom door forcefully swung open and in stumbled my daddy. He started inspecting my room and questioning anything out of place. He shouted in my face, "why is this broken?". He had noticed the damaged fire guard. I said, "me and Tom were playing daddy and I fell into it, I am really very sorry".

He didn't accept my apology or acknowledge it was an accident, instead he became extremely angry, I saw the rage building up in his face. He picked the fire guard up and swung it in my direction, I felt it suddenly hit me very hard and I naturally put my hand up to my face where it had struck me. Blood and tears were streaming down my cheeks as I felt a deep gash just under my right eye. I looked at daddy and wondered why he had just done that to me, he always reacted in the most extreme ways. I knew he had been drinking again which always made him angrier. He couldn't even bear to look at me and I couldn't get any words out to explain myself.

What he did next would haunt me for years to come though. I was picked up and thrown into the dark cupboard. I quickly realised what daddy was about to do. I started to panic as I tried to get out but he just forced the door shut, using his entire body weight to get it closed. What he didn't realise in his drunken and raging state was that my fingers were jammed as I was trying to stop the door from shutting. He locked the cupboard and I heard my daddy walking away and down the stairs.

My fingers were completely stuck and throbbing in pain. I was also pinned in a crouching position from trying to get out. I could feel my heartbeat pulsing through every single one of my tiny, trapped fingers that were jammed between the doorframe and the door. Blood and tears were pouring from my face, it was pitch black and I was sure there were mice in there. My feet were bare, and the shredded pieces of carpet were getting stuck between my toes. I screamed and screamed but no one came, how could they not hear me? For a full hour I screamed in pain, I hurt in every sense of the word. I was so distressed that I could barely breathe.

Then I heard those heavy footsteps again, coming back towards my room My mind started racing and I felt sick with all the thoughts and pain that ran through me in that moment. The key turned and I heard the lock click, it took a few forceful tugs for the door to finally open. My first words were "my fingers were stuck". Still crying my eyes out and in a state of hyperventilation I was dazed by finally seeing the light of day beaming through my bedroom window, my clothes were wet with tears and blood.

My words were completely ignored, no acknowledgement with regards to my poorly little fingers at all, or the bloodied gash under my eye which would scar my face for life.

The response to me was, "come downstairs and have something to eat, it will make you feel better. Maybe now you will learn to treat things with respect and don't you dare say anything to anyone, you don't want to be the reason this family gets split up do you? Because if that happens then it would be all your fault".

I can't explain how terrifying the cupboard ordeal was. The reason for a punishment was rarely explained, which often left me feeling very confused. This time I had been told why I deserved it though. It was to teach me to treat material things with respect, to not break things. But he had just destroyed me, he broke me as a punishment for breaking a fire guard which was an accident. What happened to me was no accident. I wasn't being treated with any respect at all. Daddy was instead teaching me it's okay to break people when they break your things, how did that work or make any sense? And why did they leave me crying for so long? I had learnt to cry silently because I would get myself into more trouble for sobbing. So the fact that I was actually screaming, I was quite literally putting myself at further risk of abuse, it should have been obvious that I was extremely distressed.

I might have only been six years old, but I could never inflict so much pain onto anybody. I couldn't understand why it was happening to me, especially by someone who was supposed to be protective of me.

I promised then that when I was older and I had my own children, I would never ever make them feel bad or sad. I knew how it felt to be the victim of such horrible actions and I would hate to be the one responsible for making someone else feel that way. I promised I would give my children cuddles and show them so much love. I promised that I would never EVER hurt them.

I never made sense of the world. I always questioned myself, wondering why I was treated in the way I was. Why didn't they see any wrong in the hurt and pain they caused? I was only a child but even I knew it wasn't right, surely they knew it too? Every time I tried to tell them I didn't think something they did was nice or right, they got really angry with me. They'd tell me I didn't know anything about life. I really didn't feel like a normal child.

No one at school liked me, I didn't have any friends. I was different to everyone else, even to my own siblings. I couldn't relate to any of the other children at school, they all seemed to be so normal and happy, they all had such lovely parents, why weren't mine like theirs? Then again, my parents were like them because Tom was okay, he was happy, my little brother and sister were too. I couldn't understand why I was so different.

At home it was a never-ending cycle, I would do or say something that upset mummy, mummy would then tell me off and then she would tell daddy, and then daddy would get really angry with me.

It was constantly on my mind that no one must ever find out what was happening to me at home, if they did the family would get split up and it would be my fault. I so often wanted to run away but I knew that if I did, it would draw attention to my family and we would be separated. Being indoors was though, most of the time, completely unbearable.

When I was just seven years old, life felt so utterly confusing. Things were so bad at home and one day I really wanted to run away. I went out the front door and got as far as the wall next to our house. I sat there, crying my heart out. A kind looking, older gentleman approached me and said, "young child, why are you so upset?". I bizarrely replied, "sir, if there is a god, then why do bad things happen to people who only ever try their best to be good?". I knew I had to be careful with my words so not to cause the separation of my family, I couldn't bear that. "Well" he said, "when you pray, you are praying to yourself, for yourself. In the name of the father, refers to your subconscious mind. In the name of the son refers to your conscious mind and the Holy Spirit is referring to your whole being. You must pray for good and good will come to YOU, does that make sense?". I nodded and thanked him whilst wiping my tears away, he asked if I was okay to which I nodded and he walked away, I never saw him again.

I attended a Roman Catholic primary school so I'd learnt a great deal about the bible and all things related to it. What he said made more sense in contrast to what I had previously learnt. He had basically just told me that God is your subconscious mind, I think I understood what he had said to a certain extent. I had this sudden sense of awareness, which would stay with me forever but I was always also trying to find the truth in his other words. I again found myself questioning myself, were my parents the way they were because they could do whatever they desired, believing that all they needed to do was ask God for forgiveness, and thus all things were then forgiven? Is this why they did what they did? Did they see no wrong in the emotional damage and physical pain they were causing? Did they even realise what they are doing was wrong? My parents weren't even religious, I think I attended a Catholic school for my granny's benefit as she was a practicing Catholic.

As you may have gathered by now, I was growing up as an extremely troubled child and was incredibly confused with life. I could see joy and happiness within my own family but it always felt like I was outside looking in at them. I was rarely invited to share the good times my family were having. What if I had of spoken the truth to the gentleman who stopped and checked on my welfare? What would have happened if I had told him that I was being abused and was too scared to go back indoors? I don't know the answer to that or what could have happened.

Even now as I write these words, I'm feeling the fear of sharing this information as it was drummed into me, from a very young age that I should never ever tell. But isn't it important to gain insight into a young mind that is suffering abuse and to gain an understanding to what's really going on? Wouldn't that knowledge help another who is in a difficult predicament?

It's a very sensitive and difficult subject. I still don't know even today if I should have spoken out because generally my siblings never went through what I did. I was singled out by my parents. My true nature is one of a people pleaser, to love and to be loved in return (I deeply craved love) to be kind and share kindness and so on. My nature just made the negative behaviour from my parents towards me all the more confusing. I never wanted to cause any harm to my family, so I continued to carry the load for the sake of my family, because despite everything, I loved them.

It wasn't bad all of the time, just most of it. On the few occasions I was made to feel like I was a part of the family, I really enjoyed it and was thankful I was being treated with such kindness. It was also better when dad was in a good mood and wasn't drinking, which in all honesty wasn't very often. Sometimes when mum was absolutely exhausted and at the end of her tether, she would ask dad to take Tom and I out for the day so she could look after the younger children and catch up with the housework and tackle the ever-increasing pile of washing.

We would get into the car and sometimes we would to head for Aberdeen, which was a sixty mile drive from where we lived. The mountainous views along the way were mesmerising to look at, this part of Scotland is extremely beautiful. As strange as it seems for someone who was born there, it was guaranteed that during every single car ride I would have travel sickness because of the altitude. I always had to take a plastic carrier bag for the inevitable sickness. If Tom and I were being loud in the car, dad would reach round and pinch me hard on the leg. I often had nail marks from the pinching, sometimes he would pinch me so hard, it would bleed. It was all done silently so no one would ever realise he had done it. When we would arrive in Aberdeen, we always headed to the fair ground, the dodgems were a particular favourite of mine. Dad would buy us some chips and a can of coke and I would always come away with a giant dummy lolly. When we were out and about dad appeared to be the doting father, times like those I thought he was the best dad in the world and wished the moment to last as long as possible. I just wanted us to stay where we were and not go home too soon, because being at home meant going back to reality.

Tom and I used to ask mum a lot if we could take our bikes and go out and play. It was different back in the early 90's, we were often out roaming on our own with our bikes. Tom had a BMX and I had a little blue bike with a basket and one of those horns which you squeeze. Tom's legs and bike were bigger and much faster than mine, I struggled to keep up with him most of the time. He would always be ahead of me, taunting me and laughing whilst telling me to keep up, I was used to him being like that so I never took much notice, although I did always try to go faster. We would also spend a lot of time playing on the park. I used to really enjoy the freedom it gave me and the amazing feelings of happiness. There was no better feeling than being carefree and enjoying ourselves. From an outsiders perspective we appeared to be a happy family and our parents were successful business owners. In reality, behind closed doors, that sadly, for me was not the case.

The business was beginning to run into serious trouble as the recession had hit hard. People were not able to afford the holidays they once did and bookings took a huge hit. Action needed to be taken but mum was trying to do a lot of it on her own whilst dad started burying his head in the sand. He was drinking more than ever and spent more time at the pub rather than at home or trying to salvage what was left of the increasingly struggling business. Before long they had reached breaking point. Mum sat me and Tom down and asked us if we should try and push through and stay in Scotland, or move to England where we would be closer to our nanna and grandad. I didn't even need to think about my response, I had only met my nanna a few times but she was such a lovely lady and I had not forgotten the feeling of safety that I had when she was around. I instantly said, without any hesitation, that I wanted to move to England. Maybe, the abuse wouldn't be so bad as we would be nearer family and I would have them watching over me. Not only that but the weather is supposed to be a lot warmer too.

The decision was unanimous and so it was decided. We were moving to England. Also, at that time if you moved from Scotland to England and were listed as bankrupt in Scotland, you could start again in England with a clear credit file. It would be a complete fresh start. They had maxed out every credit card they had on clothes and supplies to make it through, the house and business was facing repossession, they didn't have much time to get everything they needed to do organised. The atmosphere in the house was one of intense stress and tension.

My last memory from Scotland was sitting on a minibus outside of the house. The front door of the house was wide open and you could see inside that there was stuff everywhere. I know that house was left in an absolute mess for someone else to sort out. I felt sadness because we were leaving everything I had ever known, never to return again, but my feelings of relief was far greater than the sadness. We were taken to a train station & boarded a night train. It was the start of our six hundred mile journey to Southern England.

Chapter 2: Fresh Start

February 1992

We're all looking out of the train window and we are sharing a feeling full of excitement and anticipation, all of us were trying to get a glimpse of the town which was to become our new home. The land looked green and flat which is the complete opposite to the mountainous views which we had been accustomed too. I had no hint of travel sickness either, the flat land of Essex was already agreeing with me. That alone made me really happy, it was a pleasant surprise. I genuinely felt a feeling inside of me that this is home, this is where we were meant to be. As the train was slowing down the excitement inside of me was increasing, we then heard the words through the speakers of the train that we were approaching our final destination. "This is us", said mum. I was so excited. We scrambled together what we had with us and finally got off the train, that was the end of the longest journey I had ever been on. Dad hadn't traveled with us, he had to drive the rental van which was filled with as much of the furniture and belongings it was able to fit, I was curious over which possessions had made the move and what had been left behind.

Mum found the phone number for a local taxi firm on the information board and arranged us a taxi. It didn't take long at all for it to arrive. She told the driver we had just got here and that we had moved from northern Scotland. She told him that we were going to be living here but this was our first time in the town. The taxi driver was keen to show us a glimpse of the beautiful little town we had just arrived at. One of the first things I noticed was all the boats and ferries, I'd only ever seen fishing boats, but these ferries were ginormous and were stacked high with shipping containers in many different colours. The taxi driver went on to say that the port also docks cruise ships, so we'd be seeing a lot of those whilst living here. I was so glad to still be living by the sea, I will always absolutely love the sound of the waves. Even the sea itself appeared a lot calmer down south.

As we drove further around the outskirts of the town, gone were the boats and my eyes lit with pure excitement as I saw a long stretch of glorious, sandy beach. I could see two very distinctive black and white lighthouses and close to those was an outdoor skating rink and beach cafe. It was very beautiful indeed and it looked as though there was a lot for us to do and explore. As you already know I had only ever known a beach to be full of pebbles, I couldn't wait for the chance to walk bare foot on the golden sand.

The town was rather small and within ten minutes we had arrived at, 'dad's best friends house'. Prior to children, mum and dad had lived not too far away from where we were about to start our new life. It was about a forty-five-minute drive away from my grandparents. To me though it wasn't close enough. I had dreamed of a life where we would be close to them. I would have loved to have been able get on my bike and just go and visit them on my own, but that wasn't meant to be which disappointed me, I felt almost cheated. I'm guessing from my parents perspective we were close, but not too close. It left me once again thinking about how I would like life to be for my own children. I would love them to live close to family and especially to their grandparents.

My dad's friend, his wife and children were very welcoming and made us feel comfortable whilst we were staying with them. They had a beautiful garden which wrapped around the house and we spent a lot of time playing outside together. Life had seemingly, also very suddenly, taken a turn for the better. A few days later dad arrived with the van and the keys to our new home. Off we went and the mood all around was extremely positive. Finally it seemed like I was getting everything I had ever wanted, a happy family life.

The moving van was unloaded. Out came the beds, the sofa and our bikes! My little trampoline even made it, I honestly thought that would have been left behind, it had seen better days, but it still worked and was such good fun to play with. The best thing they brought was my drawing board, I absolutely loved drawing and colouring pictures. The drawing board had a space to hold a roll of plain wallpaper which you pulled over the top of the board and secured at the bottom with a metal bar. My eight birthday was two weeks after the move and I received a giant pack of thirty felt tip pens from dads friends. It was the best gift ever. I used to like drawing ladies in beautiful big dresses and wedding dresses. I thought whilst drawing them how much I would love to, one day, wear a big dress like that. I would often daydream about it, I bet they made women feel amazing and so very beautiful. When I get married I would love to wear a big fairytale dress.

Dad applied for, and got, a taxi drivers license and started as a self-employed taxi driver. Mum started working as a direct salesperson for a beauty company. She would go door to door dropping catalogues off and collecting orders. I would often walk around with her and help where I could. Because of this we met a lot of people who lived in the local area, they were all very nice and made us feel welcome, but mum wasn't making any new friends. There was a lot of walking involved in mums work, but it didn't feel hard, I really enjoyed my time helping her. As I collected the books from doorsteps, I would check the order forms and I would call out to mum, "it's another order!" or "they haven't ordered this time".

We had placements at the local Roman Catholic primary school. It's worth noting that since my encounter with the kind gentleman, I was confused if God even existed. Even so, I knew there was a lot to be learnt from the teachings in the bible. I would interpret the teachings in my own way and work out what they could mean in a modern society.

School was initially very difficult for me. I was an eight year-old Scottish girl, with a very strong northern Scottish accent. The children at the school were all fascinated by the way I spoke, but nobody could understand a word I was saying. The Southern England and Scottish accents are completely different. I remember vividly talking to a girl at school whilst washing up paint brushes and pots after an art lesson, she clearly didn't comprehend a word I was saying. She gave me an awkward smile and a nod in agreement, a response that made no sense regarding what we were talking about. I thought to myself I really need to adapt, to start talking like everybody else here. I ended up slowly losing my accent and adopting a more local tone to my voice. Tom did this too. This really disappointed my dad, being Scottish himself, he is rather fond of the accent. He definitely didn't like becoming the only one in our immediate family who spoke differently.

For the next couple of years, things weren't too bad. I do however remember the morning of my ninth birthday. Dad walked down the stairs and said to me, "I hope you have an unhappy birthday". I can't remember anything else about that day other than that, his words always stuck with me though. Who even thinks to say something like that? Well except him.

Dad had a new local so he was happy. Sometimes we all went to the pub with him as it was family friendly. Dad would always buy us a bag of salt and vinegar crisps and a coke. He also taught me and Tom how to play pool and we'd spend a lot of time playing. I used to be really competitive playing pool against Tom, and I loved winning against him. Mum didn't have the pressures of managing a business like she had done before, so she was more focused on bringing up the children. Life was pretty good and as normal, as normal could be for us.

About a year later we went on our first holiday in a very long time. It was a caravan holiday at a place called St Osyths, just a forty-minute drive away. My parents wanted us to have a holiday but one where my dad was still able to go to work as they said we really needed the money. They wanted to stop renting and to buy their own house again. Even though we weren't far from home it was such good fun. Mum said if the entertainers ask, tell them you're from Scotland! We still had a lot of our Scottish accent.

I had never been on a caravan holiday before. We went to kids club every day and I got a trophy for being very helpful. It was really good and I still remember it well. While we were there our nanna and grandad joined us, it was just for the day but they saw how happy the holiday was making us. Not long after we got home, mum had some news for us. Our nanna and grandad had bought a caravan at a holiday park in a place near Great Yarmouth. We were to share it with my grandparents and my uncle. It was the best news ever!

Within a couple of years we had moved to the upper end of town. My parents had found a new house to rent as they still hadn't saved enough for a mortgage. I was now ten years old and I was given a back door key to the house. I wore it on a piece of string like a necklace so that I wouldn't lose it. Mum had stopped selling the beauty products and started a full-time job at the local doctors surgery as a receptionist. Dad was still a taxi driver. I realised that things seemed to change, for the worse, when mum was working full time and not able to focus on bringing up us children. Someone had to look after the younger children and that someone was me. Tom was now attending a secondary school in a different town, so he couldn't do it.

In general I had been doing so well, school was going well and I was showing great potential. My teacher was always praising me for the work I was completing. I used to love getting praised at school, it would give me a great feeling of achievement and satisfaction. At home however, I began feeling as though I had the entire world on my shoulders.

A normal day was to get up and get dressed and then have breakfast, which all seemed normal enough. I would then have to walk my little brother Josh to school. He was attending a different school to myself and my sister. From there I would walk to school with my little sister, Charlotte who was now six. I would spend the day at school and I tried my absolute best whilst I was there. I loved learning and I spent a lot of time practicing my handwriting, really focusing on joining my letters up perfectly. After school I would pick Charlotte up from the infants and then walk to Josh's school, fetch him and then walk them both safely home.

The walk was a mile each way which isn't too bad, but it was in all weathers. I was a ten-year-old responsible for a four and a six year-old. No one batted an eyelid, again things were very different in those days. Once we got home, I would always make sure the house was as tidy as it could be. I would clean the kitchen after dinner and do the washing up. However if this wasn't all done to my parents standard I would be in trouble. I began feeling like I was being pushed out from being a part of the family and being treated as something else.

A lot of the time, I wouldn't be allowed to sit in the lounge watching TV with the rest of the family, if I dare to ask if I could 'come downstairs', the response would usually be, "no, get back up those stairs, we don't want to see you". Once again I was becoming very lonely and isolated. Every school day it was the same routine, but all I ever wanted was to please my mum and dad. It was getting to the point where there was never any pleasing them. Even when I wasn't asked to help out I'd offer. I used to have the job of sorting out the sock basket which had more odd socks in it than pairs, I really didn't like that job much, I wasn't allowed to remove the odd socks from the basket which didn't have a matching sock, just in case the other one would miraculously show up.

One warm and particularly sunny day, I was sitting on the front porch of the house picking lavender from the bush in the garden, I wanted to try and make some perfume. Whilst doing so I heard a voice behind me say, "hello". I turned around and saw another girl, around my age, with a girl much younger than she was. The youngest girl lived next door and was an only child. I said hello to them both. We asked questions about each other, the older girl even had the same name as me, Marley. What were the chances of that. Marley lived in the next road from me. We were talking for a long while and arranged to meet up again. I didn't know it at the time but this girl was to become the best friend a girl could wish for.

Our friendship really grew from strength to strength, and I spent time with Marley as often as I could, she made me feel so happy and normal. We used to call ourselves MnM, and we later joked we were the original Eminem! My house was by a big field and we used to spend hours making daisy chains and talking. We used to talk so much. I would sometimes go round to her house, but I was so shy. I would just stand at the doorway of the lounge because I was too nervous to go in. Marley lived with her three older sisters and her mum and dad. They were such a lovely family; they would always tell me to stop being silly and to go in and sit with them. They never knew that I felt uncomfortable because my own family rarely let me sit with them. I learnt a lot about family because of Marley, hers were so very close and all really nice people.

My parents didn't like that I was going out so much, I suppose they needed my help at home, but instead of saying that to me, they just started making it increasingly difficult for me to go out and spend time with my new friend. Marley was never allowed to come into my house and play. On occasions Marley would knock on my door only to be told to go away and have the door slammed shut in her face, but she never once gave up on me. She never ever thought bad of me because of the way my parents were treating her. On the occasions where I was 'allowed out', we would sit on the field, still talking about all sorts, normal things that normal girls talk about. We used to talk about home life a lot. I could see the sadness in her eyes with some of the stories I would tell her. I didn't realise until I saw how she reacted how bad things actually were for me at times. She kept telling me that one day I'd be free and I wouldn't be hurting anymore. I held on to the hope that one day she would be right.

There was a song which came out in the 90's and it became our song, it went as follows, 'we'll be, you'll see, yes we'll be, we'll be friends forever!'. Marley and I used to write each other letters when I wasn't allowed out, one time she wrote the lyrics to the song in one of her letters and underlined the verse which said; 'I know he's been hurting you, I've known for a while'.

Even though she couldn't relate to my experiences, she really got me and tried her best to understand. I kept every single letter she ever gave me.

Life at home became increasingly more miserable. I began to feel once again, like I was living in a never-ending hell. I would go to bed at night wishing to not wake up again, crying myself to sleep. I would cry as silently as I could as I didn't want my parents hearing me sob. Crying my eyes out in bed whilst holding a pillow over my own face was truly a terrible feeling. I felt this way every single night.

Another example is when I was asked to make cups of tea, which would be frequent throughout the day. If that tea wasn't strong enough and had a pale appearance, I would have the mug and it's boiling hot liquid thrown at me from across the room. I'd then have to clean the mess and make more tea, whilst the family are all watching me with a look on their faces as if to say 'hurry up'. I didn't like it at all when this happened, initially I'd feel the burn from the hot liquid on my clothes which would begin to stick to me and turn to a stone-cold feeling. I also felt completely humiliated in front of my family whilst clearing the mess up whilst in a state myself. That happened too many times to count, in all honesty, all the abuse I endured happened too many times, it was impossible to keep count.

How on earth could any parent treat their child that way? It was not just now and then, but on a regular basis. How could they treat their other children so differently? Who in their right mind would crush their child's soul when all they were trying to do was please them? When I had children I would never treat them this way, that was a promise I would keep forever. All I wanted was to feel accepted by my family and to be loved by them. The term black sheep certainly related. I felt that all I was to them was a live-in nanny so my parents could both go to work. Putting all the pressure on to me relieved them of their own pressures. I was seriously being taking advantage off. There was nothing I could do or say to change that and they didn't want to know or understand my feelings.

I was always being grounded after I met my new best friend. Usually I hadn't even done anything wrong but being out of the house just wasn't convenient for my parents, they used everything they could against me to keep the control they had over me.

One time I hadn't seen Marley for a while and my school netball team had a match against her school netball team, I have never forgotten about this event. I remember introducing Marley to my school friends, I had managed to make a few friends at this school, although I still couldn't really relate to them, I seemed to be more accepted. I learnt I had to mask my true self to get anyone to like me, I would never ever speak of the abuse I was receiving at home. My school friends had heard so much about Marley. It was a great feeling that they could now put a face to the name.

As it had been whilst I was living in Scotland, I didn't seem to have much in common with other children. To me they all seemed to come from much more stable homes and had parents who actually loved them.

Although I say I was more accepted within my school class, no one could fully relate to me either, they may have believed they did, but no one apart from Marley knew the real me. I used to get so much joy sitting on the school hall floor singing 'shine Jesus shine' at the top of my lungs, they were fleeting little moments of happiness. It was during moments like this that I felt the same as the other children, I felt equal to them.

I always had an awareness that the life I was living was definitely not right, what my parents did to me was wrong, and I felt that when I questioned them on my opinions, they disliked me all the more. I didn't realise at the time that everything was happening because my parents were using me, so they did not have to worry about paying for childcare or make any effort themselves towards the daily chores. Why should they? they were both working, I was living under their roof, eating their food and using water and electric that they paid for. I obviously owed them for this privilege. Realising this I knew that things were not going to change for good few years. It also gave me clarity on why my siblings lives were entirely different to mine. I was being bullied by the people who brought me into this world, I was to act accordingly and do for them all of the things which would make their lives easier, regardless of the consequences it would have on my life.

I left primary school in summer 1995. Mum and dad had arranged to spend a week of that summer holiday at our grandparents' caravan. Our holidays there were a breath of fresh air because as we were out in public a lot of the time, I was treated more like my siblings. My parents wouldn't show any mistreatment in front of anyone else, they always put on a show to others that they were these perfect parents. I lived in those moments and relished in the fun we had.

Tom and I would grab our swimming costumes and we would spend a lot of time at the pool, there was both an indoor and outdoor pool. We would roam around the holiday resort, spending a lot of our time playing on the parks and using as many of the facilities the resort had to offer. We really made the most of our owners cards. We would engage with the kids club and we entered a lot of the competitions. Myself and my siblings all collaborated together to enter the talent show. Me, Tom, Charlotte and Josh sang the song, 'uh oh, we're in trouble!'. We placed second. It was really good fun and such a funny thing to do, the audience found it hilarious. Because we were familiar faces there, the manager of the park approached my parents and said the BBC were coming the next day to do a few days filming for the 'holiday' programme. My parents were asked if they would participate in the show and be the family which would be featured. Dad wasn't sure but we all begged him for the opportunity. He eventually agreed. What an amazing opportunity it was. The following day there was a knock on our caravan door, it was the presenter of the Holiday program, the lovely late Jill Dando. She wanted to sit with us that evening at the show bar.

We were to sit at the front of the show bar accompanied by Jill and her crew. She also wanted us to join her for the day on the Norfolk broads so they could film a piece about what facilities were available to families locally. It was so incredibly exciting, not only were we at my favourite place having the holiday we loved, but we were also being made to feel like we were celebrities! Mum phoned nanna and grandad and they were so excited about what was happening so they drove up to experience it with us. I had never felt so much happiness in my whole life!

That evening Keith Harris was performing with Orville the duck and Cuddles the monkey. We had several tables pushed together at the front of the show bar. There sat my family, my nanna and grandad, Jill Dando, her crew and Keith Harris. It was an amazing night that I will never forget, I was only eleven.

The following day bright and early there was again a knock on the caravan door, we were almost ready for our day on the Norfolk Broads. Jill Dando was waiting outside in her beautiful light blue Mercedes convertible with cream leather interior, I'd never in my life seen a car like it up close. Her crew were outside in their black people carrier. We were ready to go and left the caravan. We got into dads burgundy Ford Granada and followed them to Oulton Broads, in Lowestoft.

There were two boats waiting for us and I was so excited., it was a whole new experience. I had seen boats all of my life but I had never been on one.

My family one by one boarded a boat but I was stopped from getting on, "can she come with us please?". My parents looking confused had to agree to the request. In all of my excitement I hadn't noticed that whilst my siblings were all looking lovely, well-groomed and good enough to be on the TV, my hair hadn't even seen a hairbrush, I just looked scruffy. That is why I was stopped from getting on the boat with my family.

To my utter amazement, Jill invited me on board her boat with her. It was strange that I hadn't gone with the rest of my family but I was so happy that I had the opportunity to spend this one on one time with this beautiful, amazing woman, who I had regularly seen on the TV. She was lovely and asked what I wanted to do when I grew up. She must have seen something in me because she wrote me a lovely letter on the back of one of her scripts, she told me to follow my dreams.. That letter was in the end taken from me by my dad and I never saw it again.

Jill even invited me to steer the boat. I ended up steering it straight into the riverbank, it was harder to steer than it looked so someone else quickly took back control of the boat. We ended up at a beautiful pub with wooden tables and both boats moored up so we could get some lunch. It was a perfect day and the weather was absolutely glorious. After lunch, because they had finished filming and had all of the footage they needed, I rejoined my family and headed back with them on their boat. They told me all about how much they had been filmed that day. Once we got back to Oulton Broad Jill bought us all an ice cream and then she left. She had gone to Pleasurewood Hills to do some more filming. I never saw her again. That evening, the resort manager walked up to our table and told us Jill had bought a gifts for me, Charlotte and Josh, she had requested I could have first pick of the gifts and I chose a bear called Woody, which I still have today. I will never forget the memories which were created that week, Jill Dando was a very special lady.

A few months later our episode was aired on the BBC, although my family were on the episode, I wasn't anywhere to be seen, but I took so much from that experience and was so grateful for it.

Chapter 3: Freedom

September 1995

I woke to my alarm at 6:15am after a restless sleep. Although I was tired, I felt bright eyed and excited for the first day at my new secondary school. I would no longer be able to take my younger siblings to and from school and each day I would be away from the house for much longer. All of a sudden, I felt really grown up. My parents bought me the whole uniform which was all brand new. A P.E kit, new shoes, literally everything I needed to start my high school life. I carefully dressed myself so I would look as smart as I could. I was focused and ready to begin this new chapter of my life. I was also really looking forward to seeing my old primary school friends who were joining me at the new school. The first day went well, that was once we had worked out where our form class was, the school was so big in comparison to our primary school.

One of the popular girls from primary school was in my form group, her name was Megan. Because we already knew each other we stayed together a lot throughout the day. Children came from many towns to attend this school and I made a few new friends. My brother Tom was already there, he was in year nine when I started, but we clashed a lot. Once he laid into me on the way home on the school bus and someone had to step in to get him off me. After that I ended up sitting upstairs on the bus every day and he sat downstairs. We stayed out of each other's way. I suppose with how my parents treated me that, in his eyes, his attitude towards me was okay.

I was getting older and finding it harder to keep it all together. Although initially I managed, I was beginning to struggle to stay focused on my work. It's hard to fully understand the importance of school when your home life is an absolute shambles and lacking any kind of constructive support. I know now I should have kept up my strength and focus and taken responsibility for myself. I am however only human and started to affirm a belief that if no one else cared about me, then why should I care about myself? Unless you have been there, I think it's very hard to understand. All I wanted was to love and be loved, to care and to be cared for. I wanted to do well in the long term, but when your thoughts are elsewhere, that is far easier said than done.

I had spent my short life so far trying so hard to please everybody else but when I reached thirteen, something inside me began to change. There was a group of us on the school field and someone lit a cigarette. The cigarette went round each girl one by one. When it reached me, instead of just passing it on I took a puff. By now it had a rather wet butt which, in all honesty, made it even more disgusting. Taking that puff did make me fit in a bit more with my peers though. This was the first point of beginning to change and going against my true self and my true feelings. My nanna was a smoker and although I looked up to her, I had always said I would never do it. It stinks and it's not healthy. But with my new mindset and wanting to fit in, of course I was going to rebel and start smoking, I just wanted to feel accepted. I didn't see my nanna often and once I'd had twos on a cigarette I'd smell my fingers, which reminded me of the smell of her and made me feel close to her.

On the evenings that my dad wasn't working he would disappear to the pub. On a Monday morning, because I used to be the first one downstairs, I would put my hand down the side of the sofa and look for change which had fallen from the pockets of his trousers. I would always find enough for ten cigarettes which was two pounds. I would leave the house a little earlier so I could meet Megan and we would go to the shop close by where one particular lady would sell them to us in our school uniform. She would do this as long as no one else was in the shop at same the time. I would go to school with my ten cigarettes and always sold four a day for fifty pence each. Selling them gave me enough money to buy another pack the next day.

By the time I had reached fourteen, I knew I didn't want to be doing the things I was. It was all against anything I truly wanted, but everyone I was friends with were doing the same thing. I liked being able to truly relate to other people. I liked having friends. We were starting to wear a lot of makeup and on the school bus in the morning we would glam ourselves up for the day. I became a pro at applying electric blue mascara and black eyeliner on a bumpy bus! We wore chrome silver eyeshadow and of course gold hair mascara on the two front bits of hair. I can't forget to mention the three shades too dark foundation and powder. Megan turned round to me once and said my eyebrows looked like slugs and that they desperately needed sorting out, she offered to pluck them for me. Megan got her tweezers out of her little makeup bag and went to work on these creatures on my face, I ended up with two hair thin strips "that's much better" she said!

Megan invited me to a youth club in a nearby village. Her mum, who was really young compared to my mum, ran it. I begged my parents to let me go once a week as it would be good for me to socialise and it was all very safe. To my disbelief they said I could go.

Megan and her mum picked me up, but once we got there Megan told me that whilst her mum was running the youth club, we were going to the pub down the road. I never knew that was her intention and I felt terrible that I was disrespecting and lying to my parents about where I was. I would be in so much trouble if they knew but when I got home, they didn't ask any questions and I got away with it. That made me think they wouldn't ever find out and I was happy to continue to go.

I never once went to the youth club, instead we went to the pub to play pool and smoke cigarettes. I'd cover the smell with mints and body spray. I'm still surprised to this day that my parents never found out, I still don't think they know. We met some lads there from another nearby town, most of them were only a couple of years older than us and we started hanging out every week. One of the lad's was slightly older, he seemed nice enough and he could drive. One evening at 'youth club' we asked Megan's mum if we could stay a bit later as he had offered to give us a lift home, she said it was fine. Megan was seeing one of the boys and disappeared with him for a short while. She had been telling me she was sleeping with someone but at this point I'd never even kissed anyone let alone anything else. I was happy to stay and play pool until she got back but the older lad had different ideas. He called me outside and we sat in his car talking. He then thought it would be okay to put his hand where he really shouldn't have and he kissed me. I didn't know what to do, I wasn't expecting it. This is the problem with a child, or anyone, who has been abused, you can't stop it. You go quiet and you can't move or speak. After that night I didn't go to 'youth club' again. I told my parents I didn't like it anymore and it was boring. Megan carried on going, I don't think she liked that I stopped but I told her my parents weren't letting me go anymore.

If only my parents knew what damage had been done due to the neglect and abuse they put upon me. They had no idea what they had done to me. It had so far impacted almost every single aspect of my life.

It had been a long time since my parents had bought me new clothes or shoes, my school uniform was now my brothers hand me downs. My P.E trainers were so old and worn they had no innersole and didn't fit me. I cannot explain to you how excruciating it was to walk in cheap plastic trainers with no innersoles. I would put tissue paper in to soften them before every P.E lesson but it never made a difference. I can only describe it as walking on upside down Lego bricks. My clothes were only washed once a week and I had to do everything I could to cover up the smell I must have been giving off.

Because of how I was growing up my anxiety and stress levels were high. I would sweat a lot and on hot days I wouldn't be able to take my school blazer off. My blazer was another hand me down of Toms so it too big and the wrong shape as it was designed for boys. Taking it off would reveal the sweat marks and yellowing of the school shirts, which again were Tom's old ones, and were, again, far too big for me. I used to have a quick shallow bath every morning before school but putting dirty clothes back on kind of defeated the object.

We had a fun run one day at school and I was wearing these horrible white jeans paired with a fake Giorgio Armani top. This was apparently fashionable in the nineties, well maybe not the jeans, they were awful. It was this particular day during a technology lesson that my body thought would be the perfect time to start my period. Yes I totally but calmly, freaked out. I had a quiet word with Megan who was sitting next to me and asked her if she had any spare trousers and a sanitary towel. I took my jumper off as I was wearing a strap top underneath and I tied the jumper around my waist, and then asked the teacher if I could be excused to go to the toilets. Any normal child would have told an adult but of course, I would have been in trouble. I popped the sanitary towel onto my blood-stained underwear and changed in to the trousers I was kindly lent by Megan. I tried to carry on with the day as normally as possible, including doing the 6k fun run around the school grounds, in my innersole missing trainers. I should have gone home that day and in normal circumstances I probably would have. My life however was far from normal circumstances. I was much happier to be at school and away from home, home was never a happy place. I still had to do so many chores at home, that had never stopped.

The next day was Saturday and in the morning I told mum about my period. She said she would buy me what I needed this time but she couldn't afford to buy them for me every month. She went on to say, "we can't keep supporting you financially, if you want new things and need stuff get yourself a Saturday job and buy those things you need for yourself with the money you earn".

Mum wrote a script and told me to ring around the local hairdressing and beauty salons. I rang the first one and my call was quickly answered. I read the script which was asking them to take me on as a Saturday girl. It only took that one phone call and I was offered a trial the following Saturday. I never had any interest in hairdressing and beauty as a career. If anything, I was creative and I particularly enjoyed my English and R.E lessons. The dress code the salon required was smart white t-shirt, black trousers and black shoes. I wore my school shoes and school trousers and found a couple of white t-shirts reduced to five pounds each at a local clothes shop.

The following Saturday arrived and I made my own way into town. I had to make cups of tea, wash client's hair, prepare and sanitise work tools, sweep the floor and clean the workstation after every client. I would answer the phone, take the bookings and wash and dry the towels, all the general upkeep needed for the running of a salon. It started okay and became another form of escapism from life at home. I didn't mind the job and it paid me £12 for every 8 ½ hour shift.

I walked home from work and as I entered the house mum was counting a very large sum of money. It was the money they had saved for a deposit for a house. The house which they were going to purchase was only in the next road. It was diagonally opposite Marley's house! They had already put in an offer for £38,000 which had been accepted. It was at the top of a very steep hill, with a driveway big enough for two cars. The front garden of the property was bigger than the back garden as it was on a corner. It had a sliding door porch. As you went in there was a small toilet room to the left and directly after were the stairs. To the right was the lounge and the kitchen was at the back. Upstairs were three bedrooms of a reasonable size, and the bathroom. It was exact the same layout as Marley's house.

We soon moved in and I shared a room with Charlotte. We had red and black metal bunkbeds, and I slept on the top bunk. Nanna and grandad had moved from their house and bought a caravan on a residential park and they gave us some furniture. We had an old-fashioned wooden dressing table and an old chest of drawers.

At year nine in school I should have had a good idea about what I would have like to do once I'd left secondary. Year nine was when I chose the subjects for my final two school years, the ones that would put me on the path towards my chosen career. I was already dealing with so much emotional and physical turmoil that I found it hard to even know what it really was that I wanted to spend my working life doing. I found it very difficult to know what subjects I should focus on. I had a meeting with the school careers advisor after I had started working at the hairdressers.

I wasted that meeting as I wasn't honest with the advisor or myself. I told the advisor that I already had a job and that I had a strong interest in hairdressing, I explained that I would pursue that as my chosen career. It really wasn't what I wanted to do at all. Suddenly, because of one single meeting and that Saturday job, any prospects of going to college or even university were gone. I no longer had a reason to focus on a long-term career. From that point on life was going to go from bad to worse.

I had, at some point, shown great potential at school and I knew that if I hadn't of had that job, was given the support and the balanced life that everyone deserves to have, I could have been much more successful than what my life was shaping up to become. Hairdressing is a great career, it just wasn't for me, it really wasn't my choice despite what I told the careers advisor. I wasn't a natural with hair.

It was approaching Christmas and we all helped put up the Christmas tree and the festive decorations. Every Christmas Eve I would stay up with mum and help her to wrap everyone's presents. I was given a stereo and Charlotte was given a television. When Charlotte opened her present, mum and dad said to me, "that is Charlotte's television and you are not allowed to use it". I was excited for Charlotte getting the television, but I never imagined I wouldn't have been able to watch it. They always told me to stay in our room and it was very rare that I was able to sit with the family still. Surely it wouldn't be hurting anyone if I turned the TV on?. I really didn't understand them half of the time, but I was pleased with my stereo. It had a CD and tape player and a radio. Every Sunday at 4pm I would tune into the chart show and record the songs I liked onto tape. It became a skill to try and get as little as possible of the DJ's voice recorded on to tape. I had a little Walkman and on the school bus I would listen to my recorded tapes, always sharing one of the earphones with a friend.

After Christmas dad had enough of being a taxi driver. He bought himself a white van and became a self-employed courier for a well-known catalogue shopping company. Once every six months he had the mammoth task of delivering new catalogues to all the customers in the surrounding area. Dads' delivery route spanned through three main towns. He would also deliver to all the villages and houses in between the towns. As I had a Saturday job and I couldn't help him he decided to change the catalogue delivery days to a Sunday. He said if I went with him early on a Sunday and help, he would pay me for doing it.

On the Saturday he would drive to his base and fill his van full of catalogues. That evening I'd help him sort the addresses into postcode order which, in turn planned his route. On the Sunday morning I would get up very early and go with him. When we reached the first address I would jump out of the van and leave the first book on the customer's doorstep. After that first drop, dad didn't let me get back in the front of the van, he made me sit in the back, using the catalogues as a chair. It was filthy, dusty, dirty and I really didn't like it. I could still see dad as there was a cage separating the front of the van to the back. Dad would shout out and ask for the next address and drove there. He ended up doing just the driving and I did all the manual work. It was always a long day. Dad would make one stop at a shop and buy me a chocolate bar and a can of drink and that had to last me all day. The pile of catalogues went down very slowly and I could never wait to get home.

My hands would be black from the dirt and the dust. When we finally make it home dad would pay me. My wage for all that work was £5, which even in those days was not a lot.

Mum used to like shopping for clothes from the catalogue company. She still wasn't buying anything for me even though I desperately needed new clothes so I asked her if I could order a few bits and pay her back, surprisingly she let me. I struggled to pay her back though. I was fourteen years old earning £12 a week. She was constantly reminding me I owed her which made me feel terrible. I ordered £132 worth of clothes which I desperately needed. I didn't know how I would ever be able to pay it all off.

As you know, at school I loved English and R.E, but when it came to French, that was another story. I was in the lower class and I struggled greatly with the subject. The class, as a whole, was generally a naughty one, the lowest group. Now for the most part I continued doing the absolute best I could in school, I was a people pleaser at heart, not really doing anything for my own benefit but for the benefit of not letting teachers down or giving my parents a real reason for abusing me.

It was parents evening and mum and dad went. They came back fairly late by which time I had put Charlotte,

Josh and myself to bed. I heard mum and dad come home but couldn't hear anything they were saying. They didn't come to my room so I guessed it went well. The next morning, I got up to get myself ready for school but for some reason dad hadn't gone to work.

Normally I would get up and I wouldn't see another soul as they would all still be in bed. Then I saw mum and her face, it wasn't a happy one. I could just feel something not good was about to happen. I made my way upstairs and I could hear that they were following me. This was to be the most brutal attack I was ever to receive.

They called me into their bedroom, "Miss Michoux had a lot to say about you. We have never been more ashamed and embarrassed in all of our life. We had to sit there whilst your French teacher was explaining to us what a disruptive member of the class you are and how dissatisfied she is with your work". It made a change they were actually explaining themselves before attacking me, normally there was barely an explanation for their actions. I wasn't all that bad in French, but I did struggle with the subject and I did laugh when the class clowns did something. I wouldn't have said that was disruptive to the extent they had been made to believe though.

I was on their bed with no way to escape. Dad had undone and taken off his thick leather belt which he held at the end with the holes. He then proceeded to whip me repeatedly with the buckle end of the belt, right across my back, countless times whilst I was on all fours. I ended up collapsing onto my front because of the pain. It was pure torture, these were my parents, why were they doing this to me? It wasn't just the physical pain but the emotional pain too. I loved these people, I always tried to please them but they would just hurt me, even with no excuse to do so. This was happening because of something someone had told them. I didn't even get a chance to give them an explanation. I didn't deserve to be treated like it. The whole situation literally traumatised me. My back was hurting and my head was pounding through the stress. My mind was screaming no and why, but I was not saying those words out loud. As you know, I normally cried silently but this time I was full blown bawling my heart out. My face and eyes were red and puffy, I was an absolute mess and felt in no fit state to go to school that day.

Once they were satisfied mum said to me, "thanks to you, you've missed your school bus, I'll have to take you now won't I". No remorse, no nothing. Just a lecture on the way to school and being told, like I had been before, that if I said anything to anyone and social services got involved it would be my fault and my siblings would end up in care. I would be the one responsible for splitting up the family. That was why I endured the abuse, why I never said anything. My siblings still were never treated the same way as me. They were children, allowed to be children, they had a future they could focus on. I didn't want to be the one responsible for destroying their lives.

I will never know how I got through that day at school. I will also never understand how I hid my pain and abuse; it was never picked up on. I was so good at masking myself as I had learnt the skill from a very early age. I would often hear the words, "when you're sixteen you're out, this will no longer be your home". In all honesty I couldn't wait for that day. I held on to the thought that within a couple of years I would be free and the hurting would stop, just as Marley, my best friend had previously said to me. Although it was seemingly never ending now, that would, one day, become a true statement.

For the next two years I went through the motions. I attended school Monday to Friday and worked on a Saturday. Because I was permanently grounded and not allowed out from my room, let alone the house, Marley would meet me from my school bus every day and we'd take a very slow walk home, trying to steal as many minutes together as we possibly could. The relationship with my parents was worse than ever.

I spent every single evening alone in my bedroom, completely isolated from everyone else. Don't forget I wasn't allowed to switch on the television in my bedroom. I carried on buying my cigarettes before school, which I hid through a hole in my school blazer pocket. Sometimes I would sneak out to the back garden and have a cigarette behind the shed. On one occasion, I had a pack of 20 cigarettes hidden but when I went to get one, they had gone. My mum was taking a bath so I went into her room and found them at the bottom of her top drawer. I took them back. Dad was at work and mum was having her bath, it was the perfect opportunity. Mum soon realised though and went crazy at me, she started pushing, hitting and slapping me. She didn't care if I smoked, she cared about what other people thought of her having a teenager that smoked. I wasn't then, or ever safe in that house with them.

I was coming to the end of secondary school and turning sixteen. Marley met me after school as she always did and said, "now you're sixteen, why don't you ask if you can go out, they can't keep you in forever". I plucked up the courage and asked mum and dad if I was allowed to go out. "You're sixteen now, we can't stop you". They said it very abruptly. It was not the response I was expecting but in that moment I felt pure relief. Did that mean I could now go out whenever I wanted and they wouldn't say anything? "Okay thank you so much mum and dad" was all I said, then asked what time I should come home? "Just be home for 8.30pm because you have school". I couldn't quite comprehend it, what a sudden turn of events. I couldn't wait to walk out the front door and ran across the road straight to Marley's house. "Guess what, I asked and they said because I'm sixteen they can't stop me, so here I am!". Her face just lit up! "You're free now! I told you one day you would be!". From that day onwards, we met up after school every single day. I loved my newfound freedom, no longer being isolated in that bedroom. I had my stereo and my music which really helped me through, I felt the words to a lot of songs related to me, music to me was a form of therapy.

<u>Chapter 4: The Bedsit</u>

May 2000

Now that I could go out more, I began meeting even more of Marley's friends. She introduced me to her friend Naomi, who seemed to be a lovely girl. She was so tall she towered over the both of us. The three of us decided to go for a long walk around town. As we were walking along the main road a car started slowing down and stopped beside us. There were two boys in the car, friends of Naomi. They were two years older than us, the driver, Max, had recently passed his driving test. Max and his friend, Glen, invited us to join them in the car and we had such a funny evening, it was the happiest I had felt in a long time and they all made me feel welcomed and comfortable in their company. I asked if I could be dropped off at home for 8.30pm as it was still a school night. "That's not a problem at all, of course I'll drop you off". Max, Glen and Naomi were genuinely really nice people and great fun to be around.

When I got into the house, I went to the lounge to say hello to mum but all I got from her was a glare and told just to go to bed. Would there ever be a day where I would be treated normally? Dad was at the pub so I didn't even see him. A glare from mum wasn't going to spoil my mood though, I had enjoyed myself so much that evening and was really looking forward to catching up with Marley the following day after school. I wasn't crying myself to sleep anymore and I'd start each day with an optimistic feeling that it would be a good day. Life at school was wrapping up and we were all getting ready for our upcoming G.C.S.E exams, I wanted to do well with them and was really hoping the work I had done was going to be enough. I probably should have been spending my evenings studying but I was enjoying my new freedom too much. I spent a lot of evenings out with Marley and her friends, we were so young and carefree.

Naomi and I started spending a lot of time together as Marley had begun a relationship with her new boyfriend. We would still see her a lot but she was in love! We often went out with Glen and Max in his car, they had another friend, Ross, we would see a lot too. We would spend hours with Max aimlessly driving, doing laps around town with his garage music kicking out some bad bass through the subwoofer speaker in his boot. Max would park up in the local supermarket car park and his boy racer mates would park beside him. I counted thirty cars there once. One of the funniest moments was when Max got a tow rope and tied it to his car, he tied the other end of the rope to a lamppost and done the biggest burnout anyone has ever done! The whole car park smelt of burning rubber as the car was spinning in circles around this lamppost and you couldn't see a thing through the cloud of smoke coming from the tyres. I asked Max if he would teach me how to drive and he did, I would drive around the car park and grew more with confidence the more I did it. I really thought a lot of him for doing that for me, he was becoming a really good friend too.

Max got a new car; an Astra GTE and he couldn't wait to take us for a spin in it. It was the day he got it and one of his mates thought it would be a good idea to race him whilst we were in it. They were racing side by side but approaching a roundabout, so he had to quickly get back in his lane on the right side of the road. Max hadn't got used to the handling of the car and reacted slightly too late, he smashed straight into the central island, the car spun out and we ended up facing sideways at the next exit along the roundabout. We were all ok, but the car wasn't. The front driver's wheel was bent at ninety degrees. Luckily Max's parents owned a garage and were able to recover the car quickly. He still had his old car so had to carry on using that until he repaired the GTE. He had bought it as a project car anyway so to him it wasn't a big deal and easily sorted. It taught him a lesson though and he was a much more cautious and a far better driver after that day.

It was now May and two months after my sixteenth birthday, our last day at school was finally here! I had bought some silly string in a can as it was tradition for school leavers to make a mess of the school bus. I may have gone a little over the top with the tradition because during registration the headmaster walked into my form class, accompanied by my bus driver. "Marley, collect your belongings and come with me please". In that moment my heart sank. He proceeded asking questions about the antics on the school bus that morning and as punishment I had to clean up the mess we had made. Then I spent the entire last day ever at school in the isolation room. I'd never been summoned before and now I was stuck, spending the best day I was ever going to have in school, in complete isolation. The headmaster also said he would have to have a serious think about whether he would allow me to the school prom that evening. I had taken my dress with me and had arranged to stay at my friend's house. It was just my luck after years of tradition I would be the one penalised for it.

The day was really long and seemed never ending, I was only able to leave the isolation room for break and lunch. My school friends found it absolutely hilarious, I found it far from funny. We all signed each other's school shirts and back to the isolation room I went. At the end of the day the head came back and said after serious consideration and because, for the most part, I had been good throughout my years there, I could go to the prom. I was so relieved and thanked him. I left with my friend and we headed back to hers to get ready.

The prom began with a school assembly style event where all the prefect children were given praise, then we were all led outside. We were the class of the year 2000 and as a special surprise, to mark the event, we were treated to an amazing display of fireworks. This was the first time the school had ever done anything like that. It was a really nice touch to the evening. After the firework display it was into the hall for a party except of course, my friends had other ideas. We were all dressed up and they wanted to go clubbing in town. Remember we were only sixteen, but they weren't really feeling this school event. Again, I found myself in a situation where I had no choice but to betray my parents. I wasn't really keen on the idea but because the friend I was staying with wanted to go, I didn't really have a choice.

None of us have any I.D. What if we left this perfectly good party, which the school had obviously spent a lot of money on, to go somewhere we might not be allowed into? I didn't say what I was thinking because they were all so keen to go. I knew if I called my parents to pick me up it would undoubtedly cause drama. We walked from the school into town and went to the main club in the area. I was told "just act normal, then we'll all get in". I wasn't so sure. We got to the entrance of the venue and we all walked straight in, with no questions asked. This was the first time I had ever been into a nightclub. We paid at the front desk, hung up our coats in the cloakroom and walked down the steps leading to the dance floor and bars.

I'm not going to lie, once inside it was pretty amazing! We had all walked in so confidently and now we were in no one could question us being there. I.D was the job of the door staff. We walked to one of the bars and got drinks, mine was a blue wkd, then we danced the night away. Whoever had this idea was right, it was one hundred times better than the disco at the school. We all had such a laugh that night. I dread to think what my parents would have thought. Once again I'd ended up somewhere completely different to where I said I'd be, it was worth it though. The night ended perfectly it really was a great night to end our time at school. The next day mum picked me up from my friend's house and I told her how good the school prom was, it all went without a hitch.

I left secondary school on the Friday but was yet to take my G.C.S.E exams. On the Sunday I was bored and really wanted to go out, I was enjoying this new freedom I was given. Marley was with her boyfriend and Naomi wasn't coming out, so I rang Glen to see what he was up to. He lived at the top of my road so it was easy to get to him and he was good company. Whilst I was at Glens my mobile phone started to ring.

I pulled it out of my pocket to see on the screen a call from home. I answer with a thought in my mind that dinner must be ready. Mum was on the phone, "your father and I have been talking, your stuff is in bin bags by the front door, we're throwing you out". With that, she hung up the phone. I turned to Glen and said, "that was my mum, she's just said they are throwing me out and my stuff is in bin bags". "They wouldn't do that to you, it's probably a threat, I wouldn't worry, but I would suggest you do go straight home and find out what on earth is going on". Of course he was right, how could they do that? they were a lot of things but they would never make me homeless. They were probably just going to talk to me about being out so much. I hadn't even done my exams, no way would they throw me out.

I went home, feeling really anxious, I had no idea what was about to happen. I slid the porch door open, put my key in the lock of the front door and took a very deep breath as I opened the door. When I walked in I noticed bin bags lined up by the front door. Dad came to the hallway where I was standing. "Give us your key your done here".

I was in complete disbelief, "okay dad". I looked at him, stunned. I didn't know what to think, were they really being serious? I waited for something to be said, for them to tell me they were just trying to teach me a lesson and to take my stuff back upstairs. There was just a long silence, they didn't say a word, they were indeed being completely serious. They were throwing me out. I handed dad the door key, picked up my belongings, which filled three bin bags, and walked over the road to Marley's house. I did not know what else to do.

Marley was home and she opened the door to me, "I've been kicked out, what on earth do I do Marley". By this time the tears were rolling down my cheeks. Marley's mum heard what I said and called me into the lounge. She said to me, "I have been waiting for this to happen, I knew they would do this to you, please don't cry, you're safe here and you can stay here with us, you've always been like another daughter to us". It was all feeling very surreal, like it was not really happening, but it was. I was so incredibly grateful to Marley's mum, I was in a state of shock, it had all happened so quickly and unexpectedly. How on earth could my parents do this to me? What had I done in my life to deserve it, to deserve anything I had ever endured from them? My heart was, once again, shattered. The people who were meant to love and care for me the most, didn't actually care for me at all. I loved them though, through everything. I wanted to be accepted by them, I just wanted them to love me. I stayed away from them when they asked me too or when I knew my company wasn't wanted, which was pretty often. I could never please them, they never wanted me. The first opportunity they had to get me out of their life and they took it, without any feelings or understanding of the damage they had inflicted upon me, not only now but throughout my life.

I still had my exams to do. How on earth was I going to be able to focus on them when my life was a complete mess? Marley's parents came up with a plan. They very kindly said that I could move in with them to feel safe and secure so I could focus. Then once my exams were finished, they would get in touch with the local homeless association and put in a request for accommodation for me.

This is exactly what happened, they made me feel safe, secure and comfortable. They treated me like one of their own. I could never ever thank Marley's parents enough for what they did for me. If it wasn't for them, please tell me where would I have been able to go? I didn't know about homeless associations, I barely knew anyone in the town, I had only recently met my new friends. If it wasn't for Marley's family I would have been on the streets.

After a few weeks I'd settled in at Marley's, but it was such an awful feeling, walking past my parents' house where my family were. It made me feel physically sick each and every time. It used to feel like they were watching me.

I had to start getting up early again to catch the bus to school so I could sit my exams. Even if I only had one exam a day, I had to hang around waiting for the school bus to take me home again. Everyone else had their parents running them backwards and forwards to the school, I wasn't even seeing mine let alone anything else. They had well and truly shut me out from the family. I was only sixteen, it was emotionally difficult coping with it all.

I missed one of my exams as I'd read the timetable wrong. It was the second part of the R.E exam and if I had of sat it, I know I would have done very well. Within two weeks I had completed the exams, so it was now a waiting game to see how I had done. I wasn't holding out much hope, not that it really mattered. I didn't have a plan in place to attend college or go to university. I really am disappointed that I never had those opportunities because I know I could have done so much better for myself with the right support.

I knew that now the exams were completed, my time living with Marley and her family would come to an end. I was beginning to feel really scared, wondering where I would end up, what on earth was going to happen to me. Marley had an older brother, he and his girlfriend, Marie were aware of the homeless association. Marie put everything in motion to get me somewhere to live. It wasn't going to happen overnight, but I was told I could stay with Marley until it was all sorted, so I still had somewhere to live.

I tried putting it all to the back of my mind. Marley was getting really serious with her boyfriend and she would spend a lot of time with him. When she was with her boyfriend I'd spend a lot of time with Naomi, Max, Greg and Ross. I started to become really close to Max, he was such a good friend to me, he would often pick me up and we would hang out at his parents house. He would cook me food, cheeseburgers were his specialty. My friendships with them grew so much within a relatively short space of time. They knew just how difficult life was for me under my current circumstances. They had no idea how hard my life had actually been though. I always tried so very hard to hide my sadness, I would still live in each moment and grab any chance of happiness I could get.

I had to go to Colchester to collect my exam results from school. Max took me that day and I passed them all but one, they weren't amazing results but passes nonetheless. My highest was a 'B'. Sadly I also got a 'U' which is an ungraded mark because of the R.E exam I missed.

A call was received from the local homeless association, asking for a letter from my parents confirming that I was indeed homeless. I walked across the road and knocked on the door. Mum answered and I asked her if she could write the letter for me. I was kind of hoping she would say no and ask me to come home, of course she didn't. She did write the letter so I should, at least, be grateful for that. It was that letter which secured my accommodation. There was a room for me in a bedsit right down the other end of town. I wasn't very familiar with the area I was going to be moving too. Marley's dad offered to take me there, I know it made them feel bad but they had done more than enough for me and I didn't want to be a burden to them. When we arrived we are escorted in and given a quick tour downstairs, then led upstairs to the first room, it was door number 1. The room was a nice size, there was a bed made up, a sink, kettle, chest of drawers, built in cupboards and wardrobes. I put my bin bags down and Marley and her dad left, I know they were upset. I looked around at my surroundings and realised that I was alone again. Just sixteen years old, with nothing but bin bags and a Saturday job. I was heartbroken, scared and once again isolated. All I ever wanted was to love and be loved, be a part of a happy family and home. This reality was so far away from those dreams.

Chapter 5: The Flat

August 2000

That first night in the bedsit my mind felt so tired, I don't think I had ever felt so utterly drained. I needed some time to reflect and rest. I could hear strangers walking around the house, but I kept my door locked. I had no idea who I was sharing this house with. The only thing I did know is that they couldn't have been much older than me, the charity only homed sixteen – twenty-five-year-olds. I lay on the bed and noticed there was a streetlight attached to the property, it was shining directly through my windows. The lights in my room were off but my room was lit up brightly. I'd always struggled to sleep unless it was completely quiet and dark so I wasn't sure how I would adapt to the new environment that I was in. I found it really hard to switch off, not only from my constantly racing mind but also from the new noises I could hear around me. The building was situated on a busy main road with cars constantly driving by. Through the night I could hear music blaring from the local boy racers and noises coming from the quay, which was only a few hundred meters away. I lay in my bed, awake for the majority of the night, quietly crying for most of it. I must have been so exhausted that I did eventually fall to sleep, but I didn't stay asleep for long.

The next morning when I got up I really needed to go to the bathroom, which was opposite my room. It was the only bathroom in the house. Even though it was directly opposite my room, to me it felt really far away. I was too scared to open my door and show my face. I could hear people wandering around, they were so loud so I waited until things had gone quiet. I very quietly unlocked and opened my bedsit door and peered out into the corridor, thankfully no one was there so I took the opportunity to use the bathroom. I eventually managed to get myself ready for the day, I had to go to work so had to walk through the house to get out. With a deep breath I mustered up the courage to venture downstairs and out through the front door.

The fresh air hit me like a ton of bricks. I could breathe so much better now I was out of that building. I started walking towards work, trying to pull myself together. I quickly realised that the £12 a week wouldn't be near enough to support myself anymore. I asked if I could work more hours, but it was refused. I don't think they even wanted me working there anymore. I really was a liability wherever I went and felt so worthless. It was a real blow but I knew I didn't look like the typical girl you would find in a salon. I was an absolute mess of a human being, but I needed to find a new job, and I needed to find one fast.

After work that day I had a meeting with the manager of the house, he was a very kind and compassionate man. He had done everything to arrange housing benefit for me. My weekly contribution was going to cost more than I earnt. What was I going to do? I would need food and everyday items in order to live too.

When I at school and I had the meeting with the careers advisor, I had explained to her that I would be leaving school to start a hairdressing apprenticeship. This was never, as I said previously what, I wanted to do and now I was even losing my opportunity to fulfil doing that. Marley had a job as a cleaner at a pub which she didn't want anymore and suggested I took over. It was just over £100 a week and I knew I could live and afford everything I would need on that amount of money. She had given me yet another lifeline. She had a word with her bosses on her next shift explaining she didn't want the job anymore but she had someone reliable to take over. They asked her to bring me in to talk about it. Marley phoned me, she was now staying with her boyfriend who was living opposite this pub, coincidentally he was living in the flat which was above the salon I worked in. Marley told me that she had spoken to the bosses, who wanted me to go with her and meet them. I did not have any time to waste so after my shift at the salon I went upstairs to see Marley and we went straight to the pub to get it all sorted.

Marley must have told them a lot about me as they already knew I was now living on my own and I needed more money to live on. They even added to the job role so they could pay me more. They were very understanding and genuinely wanted to help me. They offered me extra duties to build up my hours by looking after their two children for a couple of hours, after the cleaning, each day, all I had to do was make the children lunch and then take them out to the park, which would be easy for me as I'd done the same with Charlotte and Josh.

Marley went back to her boyfriend and I walked home, completely alone, to the bedsit. I told myself over and over that everything was going to be okay. In that one day I had lost a potential career but I had gained a means to look after myself, which I was extremely grateful for. I was feeling happier and decided to give Max a call to see what he was up to. "I'm not up to much, I'll pick you if you want and we'll go for a spin, I'm going to call Glen and Ross too, I'll let you know when I am on my way".

I was really looking forward to going out for a bit, I really did need it. I was hiding away in my room, still not feeling confident enough to show my face. Max picked me up after about twenty minutes, he had already picked our other two friends up. Max suggested we head out of town and grab a McDonald's. I had just about enough money for a happy meal, so that was going to be a real treat, a little celebratory meal. We went through the drive-through and Max parked up in the car park. I felt completely comfortable in their company and while we were eating I told them all how I was feeling nervous in my new home. I'm glad I shared my feelings with them because they then offered to help me with it. When we got back into town they would all come in with me. They said we should hang out in the lounge and see who it was that I was living with. I think they were nervous about the unknown too but they knew I couldn't continue to live like I was.

We arrived back in town and Max parked his car opposite the bedsit. It was strange for them to actually get out of the car and go into a building, that's not how boy racer life works. We went in, switched the lights on in the lounge and closed the curtains. There were two sofas and an old TV. They really did make themselves at home. "This isn't right at all", said Max, "we need some music! Ross, stay here with Marley, Glen, you come with me". Max and Ross went and were back within twenty minutes with a stereo system. They set it up and we were all sitting there chatting amongst ourselves. Suddenly we heard the door and another boy walked in, "hello mate", said Ross. "Alright mate, what are you lot doing here, wasn't expecting to see you!". Ross pointed at me, "our friend Marley has just moved in, do you live here too then?". "Yes mate, I live on the second floor, there is another girl who lives here but she keeps herself to herself". He turned to me, "hi Marley, I'm James, nice to meet you".

That moment gave me so much relief, especially because Ross and James knew each other. James ended up sitting with us in the lounge which looked as though it hadn't been used for a very long time. From then on, I felt comfortable and safe in the place that was now my home, all thanks to my friends. We used to see the other girl that lived in the house as she passed through, she would always say hello and smile, but I think she preferred her own company, though we did invite her to join us. We all ended up making it a regular thing, sitting together when we didn't have anything else to do, we also arranged nights out together. A bad situation turned into a good one almost instantly. I stopped waiting for silence before using the bathroom, I prepared my meals in the kitchen. I was so thankful to my friends. I don't think they ever realised just what they did for me that night. If it wasn't for them, I would have continued feeling uneasy.

My bedsit became a hub for our friends to meet up and I was rarely alone. I began meeting friends of friends. I made more female friends and before long our group was filled with all sorts of lovely young people who were just wanting to have fun and enjoy life. We discovered a cheap sparkly white wine which took effect very quickly. It was the ideal drink to have before a night out. Every single Thursday, Friday and Saturday evening we all went clubbing. On Thursday and Friday we would venture out of town and on Saturday we would stay local. Max was always designated driver, he preferred it that way and I think he took great pleasure in seeing the undesirable states we would ultimately end up in. We had a whole heap of fun. Even though I didn't have much in material form, I had never felt so content and happy, my friends made me rich with happiness. All of them, in their own way, really helped me through a time of my life that could have been far more disastrous. They were indeed some of the happiest times I have ever had.

Max's old hi-fi system was still in the lounge and that thing really kicked out the sounds. Before and after our nights out, the bedsit became a fun-loving party house! No one had to ask where to meet, everyone just knew where to go. The only problem with that was the neighbours. They did not like the continuing sound of bass through the night. I totally understand, as I too wouldn't appreciate it, but we all were between sixteen and nineteen years old with no parental guidance. The police would often knock on the door, but before long realised we weren't doing anything seriously wrong and would just ask us to turn the music down to a respectable level. For the situation we had found ourselves in, I know it could be assumed that we could have been doing a whole lot worse.

Although I had been to work, I didn't have a lot of money left out of my wages from the previous week, not even £1 making my mood pretty low. I stopped at a bakery on the way home from work because I was literally starving. The bakery sold single plain rolls with just cheese in, I thought to myself I must have enough for one of those. I went into the bakery and asked how much the cheese rolls were, the lady behind the counter said, "65p". I pulled the change out from my pocket and counted 63p. "I'm sorry I haven't quite got enough, I'll have to leave it". She must have seen me walking past a lot, maybe she knew I was living in the homeless house. She turned to me and said, "just give me what you have, don't worry about the 2p, and grab yourself a bag of crisps too". I was so hungry I couldn't thank this kind lady enough. From then on, every pay day I stopped at the bakery for a cheese roll and sometimes I'd buy one of the home-made cheese and onion pasties too, they were delicious.

Max called me one afternoon and asked if he could come round. He said he wanted to talk to me about something. I said to him, "yes of course you can, come round when you're ready". There was nothing unusual in that. He arrived shortly after but he didn't seem to have anything he wanted to talk about. We spent the evening just enjoying each other's company. I said to him as it was getting late, "I thought you wanted to come round and talk, was it anything important?". He looked me in the eye's a little nervously and said, "I think you are sometimes a bit annoying, but I can handle that, I also think your amazing, pretty, funny, intelligent and with everything you have been through, you stay strong and always seem happy. I would love it if we could start a relationship, I mean be boyfriend and girlfriend". I really wasn't expecting that at all, I had no idea he had been getting feelings for me.

Strangely I instantly had this negative feeling and my mind started telling me that he was too good for me and that I would bring him down. He deserved someone far better than the person I was. I wanted him to stay in my life. If I had a relationship with him and we didn't work out I would lose him forever and I didn't want to lose one of the best friends I had ever had. Now this is where my past had caught up with me, in that moment that I was having with Max. I had also developed feelings towards him, it was mutual, he was always there for me. I had a whole lot of love for him, but I turned him down and it was all because of the feelings of love I felt. I thought so much of him, I didn't want to put him through the burden of having a relationship with me, the liability. I didn't know how to be in a normal happy relationship because I didn't feel like a normal person. That was another big mistake in my life. I wish so much I didn't think so negatively of myself, I wish I had told myself I am good enough, I do deserve to be happy, but I never did tell myself any of that and I let him go.

I didn't and couldn't see my own worth, I couldn't see what others could see. I was this young girl who had overcome extreme adversity in her life, I was strong and very determined, but I still also had this niggling feeling of 'if no one cares then why should I'. All I had ever wanted was the love and acceptance of my parents. I never once wanted my life the way it was now. The only reasons why my life had so far become this way was due to the circumstances which were surrounding it. If only my mindset had been different, but at that time I was right, I felt like I was as an extremely damaged individual.

It was coming up to Christmas and all my friends were telling me what they had planned for Christmas Day, I asked if any of them would be around but every single one of them said no, they would be spending Christmas with their own families. It was becoming increasingly likely that I would be spending Christmas Day completely on my own in my bedsit, at just sixteen years old, I was still so very young. I only had one option left, to phone my parents and ask if I could spend Christmas Day with them. They were still my family and I was still their daughter. I picked up my phone and dialed the home number, mum answered. "Hi mum, it's me, would it be ok if I come and spend Christmas with you all?". "Yes of course you can, we will come and pick you up Christmas morning", "thank you mum, I am really looking forward to it". I came off the phone so very surprised that she had actually said yes and not only that, but had offered to pick me up too. It felt really good to know that when I was asked what I was doing for Christmas, I could now answer like everybody else, by saying I'd be spending it with my family.

With my next pay packet I went to town and bought all my family a gift each. I left myself with no money whatsoever, but even though I was leaving myself struggling it felt like it was a worthwhile thing to do. I wrapped and labelled all their gifts and put them in a carrier bag ready for Christmas Day. The day soon came and I got up really early feeling quite happy. I had no idea what time they were picking me up. I went to the bathroom and had a shower. Then I went back into my room and put on the nicest clothes I had, I did my hair nice, put on my makeup and I was ready by 8am. They hadn't phoned yet to say they were coming but I was sure they wouldn't be long. I sat patiently waiting, all on my own on Christmas Day. The hours went by and my thoughts started running away with themselves. I was beginning to feel really worked up and sad for myself. It really wasn't nice. It got to 2pm, and I thought to myself that they weren't coming for me, maybe I should ring them. I nervously picked the phone up, I was scared to actually make the call, but I really didn't want to spend this day alone. I hated being alone, especially today.

I make the call and mum answered, "it's me mum, what time are you picking me up?". "No, we can't pick you up, everyone has had a drink. If you want to come here, you will need to make your own way here". "Ok thanks mum, I won't be long".

I didn't notice that they didn't actually want me there. I forgot that I was rarely part of the family even when I lived with them. I just didn't want to be on my own. I lived a two mile walk away so I would have to walk four miles that day just so I wasn't alone. I walked as fast as my legs would take me. They had already had their Christmas dinner and opened their presents when I got there. I overlooked all of that though and was just grateful they didn't say no. They didn't seem to like their gifts, but it was all I could afford, I couldn't even afford to spend what I had spent. I had been there for a couple of hours when Max sent me a text message asking if I was okay and if I was having a nice Christmas, he said he was picking Greg and Ross up and I was welcome to join them. Knowing I was, at the moment, in the company of people who didn't even want me there. I texted him back asking him to pick me up from my parents, I didn't say I had spent most of the day completely alone. I'd rather just forget about that bit. I wished my family a happy Christmas and left them to it. At least that Christmas finished on a good note, I was always happy when I was with my friends.

After fourteen months of living in the bedsit the house manager told me that I needed to move on. I was now seventeen years old. Where I was living was only temporary accommodation and I had gone over the twelve-month tenancy agreement. The manager helped me a lot and he arranged a flat for me with another local housing association. This flat was situated in one of the roughest streets in town. I had found my parents to be slightly more approachable and I told them what was going on. I also asked them if they would view the flat with me, which they said they would. I met them outside the flat the day I was going to view it. The block looked alright from the outside, it didn't look rough, it was in town near all the shops. Whilst we were there I told my parents that I liked the flat but I would much rather move home with my family, all my friends still lived at home with theirs. They said they would let me know the following day.

The day after, mum rang me, "dad and I have spoken about you moving back home and we have both decided that we don't want you to move back in so I strongly suggest you take the flat". Why had I once again given them an opportunity to break my heart, I don't know why but it really hurt me hearing mum say those words. The flat was now my only option, I suppose it always was going to be my only option. I contacted the house manager and thanked him for everything he had done for me and told him that I wanted to take the flat, so please could he let the housing association know. I started getting ready to move out of the bedsit that held so many fun and happy memories. I got all my belongings together and carried them down to the lounge. Max and my other friends helped me move my stuff to the new place, but they really didn't like the area and didn't want to hang around for too long. I kept asking them all to pop round but they never ever wanted to. They would only come and pick me up from outside, they never wanted to come in. It was definitely the area putting them off. It made me really sad and I started to feel incredibly lonely again, we had built up such a good life in the bedsit and now things were totally changing once again.

Chapter 6: The Shift

February 2002

The flat had been fully decorated prior to me moving in. The housing association had laid new carpets, light beige brown ones. They weren't the soft fluffy one's, but the firm hardwearing type with the lines in. The walls throughout had been painted a light pink but the bathroom was a Crayola green. It was awful, I'm really not a fan of green, but regardless, it was mine, my own space which I did not need to share. The flat had a small bedroom at the back and the bathroom was opposite the front door. The lounge and kitchen had a partition wall which divided the two to make them appear like they were separate rooms. It was a very decent living space for a seventeen year-old and I felt incredibly grateful that it was my flat. I bought a cheap kettle, toaster and hoover. My nanna and grandad sent a double bed for me. One of my friends parents were getting a new sofa and offered me their old one, to my surprise, dad said he would pick it up in his van and put it in my flat for me. Dad also bought me a very small portable TV, I gratefully accepted it all. I was beginning to have everything I would need.

When I needed to do a small food shop for myself, there was a supermarket right at the end of the road, it was literally a 100m away, if that. It was nice that I now had my own kitchen area that I didn't need to share with other people too. I managed to get a washing machine and I would dry my clothes over the radiators or on a clothes airer. I wasn't exactly big on cooking myself big meals, I was generally living off beans on toast or jacket potatoes with cheese. I didn't get much satisfaction cooking for myself and didn't feel it was necessary.

I was coming home from work one day and I bumped into my neighbour for the first time. He lived in the flat directly underneath mine. He wasn't much older than me, the same age as my older brother in fact. He seemed a really nice person. He invited me into his flat for a cup of tea and a chat. He had also experienced many troubles in his life but had an optimistic attitude, much like mine. I liked that and I liked him, he always had a lot to talk about and I really enjoyed his company. After our first encounter I would pop in for a chat literally daily. I met one of his friends, Ellie, she was a nice girl and told me about a day trip she was going on to Alton Towers. She told me how much it was and invited me to go and to also ask if any of my friends would like to book, as there were still lots of spaces available. I messaged Max and told him about it, he wanted to book and was going to ask the others. A few of us ended up booking. I was so excited. I had never been to a big theme park before and everyone kept saying Alton Towers was the best in England.

The trip came around so quickly. The night before I could barely sleep, I was so excited. We had to catch the coach at 4am. I set my alarm for 3am and at 3.30am everyone who was going in our group started knocking on my door. I had recently bought new trainers, they were Nike and were super comfy, I'd never owned such a nice pair of trainers and was keen to show them off. I wore bootcut jeans and a black strapped top. I wore my hair half up and half down. I was feeling fantastic and full of excitement. The pickup point was at the end of our road and before long the coach arrived. I sat next to Max. One of my friends from secondary school, who lived in a different town, ended up on the trip too, she knew Ellie because she worked with her, what a small world it is! We had the most amazing day out. We went on the oblivion twice and the black hole twice. There was a new ride called air and me and Max managed to get on the front row! That ride was awesome! The funniest moment had to be the haunted house, I even bought the photo of us all on the ride because that, on its own, was hilariously funny. You could just see the fear in everyone's faces! It was an absolutely brilliant day and I really didn't want it to end, but of course it had to. We got home about 10pm and by then everyone was ready for their beds. I slept very well that night.

Max had finally finished restoring and repairing his Astra GTE, it was now an absolutely stunning car. He had a great eye for detail. It had tinted windows, a new exhaust system, alloy wheels and he'd had the body work sprayed a deep dark metallic purple. He had fitted a top of the range sound system; the entire car was immaculate. Max had been helping to build a website for a well-known car event which was held at Arena Essex Raceway on the last Saturday of every month. He invited me to go with him most of the time. We would head up to Greys and would always be stage side in the arena because of his links to the event organiser. I felt like we were VIP's when we there, that in itself was a great feeling. There would be shows of stunt cars, rows upon row of the most modified motor's, some of which were mind blowing. Max entered his car into the best dressed competition and won! His car ended up being featured in a couple of modified car magazines.

Once the event was over everyone would go back to their car and there would be the longest convoy of modified motors all heading for the same place, Southend seafront. So many people would perfectly park their cars side by side along the main strip right on the seafront. Everyone being socially friendly and complimenting each other's cars. Even the police would get involved with the banter, one even let me wear his hat and sit in his police car. It was all good harmless fun.

One day Max told me he was moving to a town fifteen miles away. He was starting a new job and had found a house he was going to buy there. I could never tell him how I really felt about him, but I was so happy for him. Things were going really well for Max which was exactly what he deserved. I knew we were now moving in completely different directions and all the good day's we had spent together were sadly now coming to an end.

One evening whilst I was sitting in my neighbours flat, his friend Jack showed up. I had never met him before, he was a good-looking guy, very mild and calm in his mannerisms. I was drawn to him and we instantly connected. He had also experienced troubles in his life. Jack started talking about his mum whom he was close too, she had sadly passed away two years earlier. Tragically, she died in the flat they both lived in. He found her in a chair in the lounge, not breathing. It absolutely devastated him. He had also lost a brother shortly before that in a house fire. He was broken inside and understandably so. My heart hurt so much for him. Suddenly everything I had been through seemed so trivial in comparison to his experiences in life. I thought to myself we have both faced adversity, maybe we can help each other get through it. After a while our relationship grew stronger, but he was also clearly in love with his ex. She wasn't interested and I don't think he knew at that time what he wanted. Jack would tell me he was coming round, but quite often he wouldn't show up. When he did come round, he was nice company and I enjoyed spending my time with him.

I needed a change, it was proving a lot more expensive living in the flat in comparison to the bedsit. I was now at the age I could obtain a driving license so made it my mission to achieve that goal. I deserved that at least and I knew if I wanted it badly enough that I would, and could, accomplish it. I needed a new job with better pay so I could afford what I wanted and needed. I turned eighteen and approached a really popular pub in town, asking if they had any bar work available. After a very brief interview, during which the member of staff made me laugh and I very loudly snort laughed, they offered me a full-time position. The only problem was that the pub was the other side of town, so I would have to try and get lifts, as frequently as possible, because it would work out really expensive booking taxis twice a day. I really wanted my own car. Every Friday I would be given my wages in a small brown envelope with the details of my wages written on it. I requested to work the day shift on Friday's so I could book a driving lesson from my work place whilst having the funds I needed to pay for it. Technically I was also driving myself home every Friday, which felt great. I booked my theory test and scraped a pass on my first attempt scoring 30/35. After twelve practical lessons I booked my driving test. My instructor tried telling me I was not ready for it but I was not willing to listen to him. I knew I could do it. I had a strong belief in myself, I knew which areas I needed to work on and requested we focused my lessons on those areas. Test day came and I had my final lesson on the drive over to the test centre, I took the test and passed first time. It was a massive sense of achievement, I did it and I did it on my own, with no help from anyone.

I was beginning to spend more time with Jack, he was still very unreliable with his promises of coming to see me, but I did see him, more often than not. Jack was soon to be getting a new car and had agreed I could have his old one on a pay weekly basis. It was a beautiful blue Ford Escort, with pepper pot alloy wheels and a big boys cherry bomb exhaust system. It was a sporty little thing and I absolutely loved it. Within two weeks of passing my driving test I was on the road in my very own car. I was really enjoying my newfound independence. Things became a whole lot easier for me once I became mobile with my car, I could easily get to and from work. I used to hate walking at night on my own, I'm sure that feeling stemmed from when I was five years old and walking home after the Halloween party. I always had a sense something bad would happen to me. Working the late shift became a much more pleasant experience as I wasn't feeling as vulnerable as I previously had.

With all the focus on my car I had fallen behind with my rent on the flat, I had ended up in arrears of over £600, which, now when I think about it, could have been easily sorted. However, at the time I buried my head in the sand and when letters came through, I disregarded them. I missed correspondents from the housing association chasing the money for the rent and I missed a court summons letter. I woke up one morning and left for work, a lady was outside the block of flats and asked if I knew a Marley. I said I had no idea and didn't know her. I got in my car and went to work knowing I had just made a big mistake. Whilst I was at work the same lady showed up about two hours later. She said "why did you lie about who you were, why didn't you say you were Marley?". I was scared, I knew I was facing big problems with my home, but I didn't realise how serious it was. "We're evicting you with immediate effect, I suggest if you want any belongings you come with me now to retrieve them". I called my boss down and explained I needed to go, he said he would cover me whilst I was gone but I must go back to work as soon as possible. I made my way back to the flat, the locks had already been changed and there was an eviction notice was on the door. I had two hours to get what I could out and find somewhere else to go. I called mum. She had separated from my dad the week before. Social services had started getting involved with the family, I never knew the full details, but it can't have been good. The problems of their relationship were no longer pinned on me though as I hadn't lived with them for coming up to two years. She had upped and left him and was renting a property not far from the pub I was working at. Mum suggested I go to the home I was thrown out of by them and stay with dad as he was still living there. Dad had taken the separation badly and had moved the mattress from his bed in his bedroom, downstairs and was sleeping on the living room floor. He just couldn't bear sleeping in their bedroom now mum had left him. Dad was drinking more than ever, but he would get up really early for work and would drive his van with extremely high alcohol levels within him. He did, very reluctantly, let me move in. I had to grab as many of my belongings within the two hour time frame I was given, I left so much of my stuff behind. Once I had salvaged what I could from the flat I drove back to work to continue with the remainder of my shift. That was really difficult to do as my head was all over the place, because I had ignored all the letters, I had no idea when I got up that morning what was going to happen, I was in a state of shock and felt like I had seriously let myself down.

That evening I reflected on the turmoil of the day. It was a strange feeling being back in the house that I'd previously lived in with the rest of my family. The place where I knew I wasn't really welcome. I tried to stay away from the house as much as possible. Dad's behaviour and mood were very unpredictable. He took to online dating and quickly moved on, he met a lady in Suffolk and very rarely came home. The house was going to be repossessed but for now I had a roof over my head. I felt like the lady of the manor with my car on the driveway and this three-bed house to myself. The house became a doss house for a while. Everyone who was anyone would randomly show up as word got around town that my parents were not there anymore. It did not last long though and the house needed to be cleared. I didn't know what I would do once the house was gone. I knew I had to ask mum and see if she would she let me move in with her. I asked and she said I could have the box room, all it could fit was a bed but I was grateful and felt secure for the first time in a long while.

Jack lived in a village about eight miles away and I ended up spending most of my free time there with him so I wouldn't be with mum too often. It just never felt right. I had never really had what you would call a home as you know.

I was getting really mixed-up signals from Jack. He continuously blew hot and cold, but I was falling in love with him, it felt, to me, like we were made for each other, but the more I tried the harder it got. It was almost as though he did not want me but also didn't want anyone else to have me either. I was becoming more aware of a nature in him that was more hostile than calm. I was becoming more emotionally involved, not blaming him for the way he was but, the circumstances surrounding his life.

One day we had a serious argument, something was clearly wrong, but he wouldn't talk to me about what was actually bothering him. Instead, he made me feel worthless and insignificant. He got so angry with me for trying to get him to tell me what was wrong, that he grabbed me by the jumper I was wearing and slammed me against the glass door in his kitchen. The glass shattered as my body slammed against it, but luckily enough Jack still had a hold of me and quickly pulled me forward, which in turn stopped me from falling backwards onto the large shards of glass sticking out from the window frame of the door. It could have easily been a lot worse. It shocked Jack and he could not apologise enough. I thought maybe that gave him the scare he needed to sort himself out. That was just the beginning though. Another time he squeezed my hand so hard it fractured my index finger. He told me to go home so I jumped in my car and sped down the narrow country lane which was opposite his house. I almost had a head on with a van coming in the opposite direction. It scared the living daylights out of me as I quickly had to steer my car into the hedged verge. I was lucky that both mine and the other drivers' reactions were as quick as they were. I turned the car around and headed back to Jack, I was shaking like a leaf. I told him we needed to sort things out, that we couldn't carry on like this. I don't think he believed me when I told him I nearly had a serious accident, I'm sure he just thought I was just looking for an excuse to come back and stay with him. I genuinely cared for Jack and again let things go because I felt so sorry for him. I felt at that time he was just angry with life and if I let him take it out on me it would help him. He did scare me sometimes though, and I started staying with mum more regularly, but not really showing my face much whilst I was at her house. I would either be out or hide away in my room.

Jack's attitude towards me was becoming increasingly controlling. He soon made it obvious that he did not like the fact I worked in a pub. He would question me on who I had been speaking too or who I had seen. I would talk to him enthusiastically about a shift and he would turn on me. I wasn't even doing anything wrong, all I was doing was my job. Sometimes he wouldn't even talk to me at all after work and he would always make me feel bad. Quite often I would be invited to stay behind to socialise with the other members of staff but I couldn't even do that because Jack wouldn't like it. So many times people would ask me why I was with him, but they didn't know him like I did. I knew he didn't mean any of it, it was just because he was taking his hurt from his past out on me.

Eventually enough was enough and I could no longer take the accusations and him being the way he was with me anymore. You're probably thinking 'it sounds toxic, I'm glad you got of that relationship'. What I actually did was look for another job. I loved the job I had but working evening shifts was what caused the problems in my relationship, or so I thought. I enquired about a job at a local hotel and restaurant and was given a role of barmaid, full time along with waitressing occasionally. I was employed on a day shift basis.

My relationship with Jack didn't improve with my new job, in fact, it got worse. I wasn't skilled in anything so getting a job in another sector wouldn't be an easy thing for me to do. A big chain retail store was soon going to be opening in the town and the training days were being held at the hotel where I was working. Whilst I was working behind the bar, the manager and deputy manager from the retail store were on a break from training, they both came to the bar to order some drinks. They then asked me if I would like to go and work for their company. It came completely out of the blue, I hadn't asked for, nor had I applied for a job. I must have given a good impression with regards to how well I worked. I thought about the offer, it would be away from the hospitality which I was used to, the hours were always going to be daytime. It was for a very large company. I felt really lucky to have been asked and given this opportunity. At the end of the day, I accepted their offer. I missed all the training, but they were confident I would pick the role up quickly. I was feeling really excited about starting a new job and quickly let my boss at the hotel know that I would soon be leaving.

I left on a Thursday and the grand opening for the new store was on the Friday. I got up and put on my brand-new uniform along with my name badge, I felt so good wearing it, I hadn't worn a uniform since I was at school. I met lots of new faces that first day. When it came to opening the store, I held one end of the red ribbon ready for our first customer to cut. The local press were there and we had to hold the pose for a quick photo. I was put on the tills, which I was really happy about as I could sit down all day. Most of my colleagues had the job of running around the warehouse collecting the items that people were ordering. I was really enjoying the job. I was often on customer services too as I felt really confident with being on the shop floor and I loved helping people. I made a good friend that day, Lara, we spent our lunch breaks together and we would often meet up outside of work.

Jack seemed to approve more of my new job, he was no longer having words with me about who I was talking too throughout my working days, I wasn't getting so much of the silent treatment now either.

One day, whilst I was working, Max came into the store. I hadn't seen him in a long time since he wasn't living in the area anymore, he said to me, "I didn't know you worked here, why don't you get a job with my company?". My lack of self-worth came into play again, this is Max we're talking about! He was working for a well-known communications company where only well-educated and respectable people work. "How am I able to do that Max? I couldn't do that, I don't think I'm good enough". "Of course you're good enough, you would be an asset to the company, I have just been watching you work and you're great!". Max then proceeded to tell me all about the perks of the job, which were incredible. It sounded like an amazing job to have and a great company to work for. I wasn't getting many perks where I was and, as much as I loved the job, I knew it would be another step up. Max offered to write me a C.V and arrange an interview for me. I agreed and left it with him.

Within two weeks I had an interview. Max had written the most amazing C.V and it was all true, everything I had done so far actually looked pretty good on paper. I really couldn't see what others were seeing in me, but I trusted his judgment. This was going to be the first formal job interview I had ever had, and I wanted to make sure I looked the part. I certainly didn't want to let Max down. I bought a cheap, but very smart suit, got into my car, drove the forty-five minutes to the interview and I just went for it. I wasn't holding out much hope, there were quite a few people waiting to be interviewed, why would they pick me over any of them? Within hours I had a call, offering me a position. I couldn't believe what had just happened. I wrote and handed in my notice to the retail company and took a giant leap into the world of communications, not entirely confident in my ability but trusting in Max and his opinion of me and my potential.

Now if I had not taken the steps I had prior to this, it would never have been possible, after all I was living in a small town with very few opportunities. Having a car, a driving license and most of all, the friend I had in Max gave me something in life I didn't think was possible. It was a real career, a far cry from cleaning pub toilets which I had been doing a few years prior. Now I had a job with benefits and a good income. Onwards and upwards!

I was given a position within the company in a different county to where I currently lived, but I loved driving, so it wasn't a big problem, in fact, I looked forward to my drive every morning. I had the hope that I could, in time, apply for a transfer to another branch as Max had explained to me all I had to do was get within the company. Once in I could apply for a transfer as other job positions became available closer to home. I found the job a lot to take in initially, there was a lot to learn and I had a lot of responsibility. I passed the probation period and I was given the keys to the branch. I was selling mobile phones and I was loving it. Being the first to get your hands on new technology is a pretty good place to be for someone as technologically minded as I was, it was really exciting.

I would leave home early and grab a breakfast on the way to work every morning, that was always enough to keep me going throughout the day. The incentives within the job were fab, one day our branch scored so high we were all given a piece of Tiffany jewellery. I received a bracelet which I still wear today. I had a sense of pride working there and the job satisfaction was unreal. My colleagues were more like friends. As respected as the job was it was not what I had expected it to be. I felt like I fitted in really well and I belonged within the company. I surprised myself with my ability, Max was right to encourage me into this.

Max worked at a branch in another town, but he regularly emailed me on the internal work system, sending me useful information with things that would help me to do the job well. We had a lot of banter between us. When other branches needed cover, I would willingly offer to drive over to help them out, I felt that brought me more respect within the company.

Once a year the CEO would have a huge party for each and every member of staff. Travel was paid for as the venue would always be in a well-known location within London. Drinks were free all night but prior to the event we were always reminded it was a marathon and not a race. There would be headline acts, famous DJ's, food everywhere and one year there was even a fairground within the venue. It was an absolute blast. It was definitely my most favourite perk of the job. Jack obviously wasn't a fan of this annual event, but it was such good fun that any grief I would get because of going was always worth it.

After a year of working for the company, I requested a transfer over to Max's branch as a position had become available. My transfer request was accepted and I was finally working that little bit closer to home and best of all, working with my very good friend.

With my new job and increase in earnings Jack began controlling himself better around me, maybe that was because I was now paying out a lot for him. I was pretty much staying at his full time and spending a lot less time at mums home, although I still had my room there. We were living at Jacks dads house, which wasn't exactly a clean or nice environment, but to me that didn't matter. All I wanted was to be able to spend time with him. Material things in life had never meant a lot to me, I hadn't really had much in the way of material things. What did mean a lot to me was when people showed they wanted me in their life. That's how Jack was making me feel now. We were getting on better than we had before and I had let go of the issues which we previously had. He was working as a yardman at a scrap yard, but it didn't pay much. I found my wages being drained into funding the both of us, but I didn't mind that, as long as we were a couple and together, nothing else seemed to matter. I was up early every day for work and went back to Jack every evening. Things were okay for a while but slowly life began to change. We were not saving any money and affording the costs of getting to and from work were becoming a real stress, especially when it had been three weeks since my last pay day, I was working on a pay monthly basis.

Jack did not really know a lot about Max, I had kept that to myself. I suppose I knew Jack wouldn't like it and it would give him a reason for making my life hard. If he knew I would probably have to give my job up like I had to do when I was doing the bar work. He certainly didn't know we were working in the same company let alone the same branch. Working with Max everyday gave me a lot of joy, it really made me happy. We worked extremely well together. We were very professional, but we also had a lot of banter between us.

Max had been one of the best friends a girl could ever have. Whilst I was living in the bedsit, he made my life the best it could possibly have been and he also got me into this incredible company, it barely felt like I was working at all, I enjoyed it that much. Max was my branch manager and he promoted me to a senior role within the branch. He always seemed to bring the best out in me. I was aware he still had feelings for me, he would have girlfriends, but we just never discussed them. I still felt he deserved better than me. I was so tied up in my relationship with Jack, which I knew hurt Max, and that was the last thing I wanted to do, he had always shown me so much kindness.

Max decided he was ready to leave the job and take over managing his family's business, I found this hard to deal with as I really enjoyed our time working together. I knew him on both personal and professional levels, it was a real blow. It was never quite the same working for the company without him but, I carried on as I had made many good relationships within the business and was now a well-established and respected member of staff.

Chapter 7: Imogen Lily

August 2007

Life with Jack was growing increasingly intense, we had been in a relationship for five years now and he had this hold over me, I loved him, but life was never easy with him. Jack had a 'life owes me' attitude, he did not seem to understand the concept of taking responsibility for himself. He lived his life blaming the past for the way he behaved and the way his life was. I was now twenty-three years old and beginning to feel the need of wanting to start my own family. I had not taken into consideration the life I had now and how that would impact my own children. The life you choose is the life you will potentially be bringing your own children into. Just writing those words makes me think of the song lyrics, 'If you tolerate this, then your children will be next'. Which is such a true statement. When you're still relatively young and have grown up in a dysfunctional environment, simple facts easily slip the mind. Everything I had told myself that I would or wouldn't do to my own children, seemingly had not been in my thoughts during the more recent years.

Our home wasn't exactly habitable, but I accepted things for the way they were. It was just me and I didn't matter that much. This stems back to the fact that I didn't really have much care for myself, I had settled for a relationship which wasn't really working but I still had an optimistic outlook on life. I felt that we were both still young and could heal and grow together. Jack's dad was selling the house and so we moved into a flat at the scrap yard. The building used to be a pub and the flat was on the first floor. It had recently been renovated and was a lot better than where we had been living. Other than the flat, the rest of the building was in a very poor state, to look at you would assume the entire building had been left derelict. The grounds and the building itself were extremely dirty and unkempt, rats roamed throughout the property. It wasn't a particularly inviting place but the flat itself was, in comparison, in a good way, and we were lucky to have it.

Just as we had moved in, I had a phone call from my mum, she said that my grandad had been taken ill and was in hospital. They had found him to be riddled with cancer, sadly he didn't have long left to live and it would be unlikely that he would ever be able to go home again. Over the following weeks we would often drive over to sit with him and comfort my nanna. I hadn't lost anyone close to me before now. I found it really difficult emotionally, it was so sad to see my grandad in such a frail condition. He was always so kind and gentle. He was not a man of very many words, but you just knew he was taking everything in. He sadly passed away, but I was content that I had my chance to say my goodbyes to him. Nanna was living independently and I would often drive over and sit and talk to her for hours. She was coping really well with the loss of grandad, but she needed the extra support.

After the loss of grandad, the feelings of having my own children grew even stronger. My nanna had always said that she wanted to be around to meet her first great grandchild and her words stuck in my mind. We decided to start trying for a baby right away. Months passed but nothing was happening, I wasn't getting pregnant easily. I would buy pregnancy tests but get a negative result and almost every time my period would start the next day. Each month I felt an immense feeling of disappointment, what if I just couldn't have any children? That thought alone was devastating. We kept trying, living in the hope that we would one day get that positive test. After 8 months of trying to conceive, it all suddenly changed.

I went to work one morning and came over feeling really lightheaded and slightly sick. My colleague suggested I go and buy a pregnancy test. It was a quiet day at work, so I popped to the pharmacy. Back at work, I went to the toilet to do the test. I couldn't wait the whole day, I needed to know there and then. Within a minute I saw two lines appear! I couldn't believe my eyes. I was actually pregnant. I fell in love in that moment, I also felt a rush of other emotions that shook me up. I had never experienced such a surge of different feelings my life. I just couldn't concentrate, my focus on work that day had gone in an instant. I asked my manager if I could go home early as it still wasn't a busy day in store.

Jack was working in the yard, and I phoned and asked him to come into the flat, telling him I needed to talk to him about why I had come home from work early. He came in, his face and hands, as always filthy black with oil, as were his work overall's. He looked at me with his piercing blue eyes and asked what was going on. I could not contain my excitement, "Jack, I'm pregnant!". His face lit up, he was genuinely pleased, "I'm going to be a dad!". "Yes! And I'm going to be a mum!". We were both absolutely delighted. Maybe now life was going to get better.

Over the following weeks I became increasingly unwell but I knew about morning sickness and put it down to a side effect of the pregnancy. I wasn't letting it stop me from working, I had a spring in my step regardless of how I physically felt. Everyone who goes through pregnancy carries on with their life as normal, I wasn't going to be any different. I went to the doctor who confirmed my pregnancy and the first scan was arranged. It felt like an endless amount of time to wait but, in reality, it wasn't long before the twelve-week scan came around.

On scan day we made our way over to the maternity unit for the very first time, the feeling of the pregnancy suddenly became real. The maternity unit was very busy, full of so many other couples, all looking so happy whilst anxiously waiting for their names to be called. I sat in the waiting room with Jack just taking in this amazing atmosphere that surrounded us, it felt so surreal. We waited forty five minutes and then my name was finally called. Jack and I went into the room where the scans were done. I was full of excitement and anticipation, we were about to see our baby. How amazing is that?

This was our first pregnancy so I didn't quite know what to expect. The heartbeat was strong and the baby was measuring twelve weeks, we were given a due date of the 19th May 2008. The lady doing the scan said she just had to take a few measurements then she went really quiet. It's just routine I thought to myself whilst staring at the screen, she then looked at us both and calmly said, "the measurement at the back of the neck is measuring a little thick, it may be a sign something is wrong, possibly Down syndrome. All it takes is a simple blood test and we'll know if it is or isn't". I was then given the photograph of our baby scan before we were asked to go to antenatal to have some bloods taken.

I walked out of the room so confused, I noticed again all the happy couples waiting to be seen, but my smile had gone. I had imagined and expected the scan to be a lovely experience. Why did it have to be my baby? My feelings now were very different, I was so scared. I hadn't even considered that anything could be wrong. Of course, I was upset but I also knew I loved this baby, if it had Down syndrome we would handle it. What's an extra chromosome anyway? I was strong enough to be strong for our baby.

Within a week a letter came with the results. It was negative, our baby didn't have Down syndrome. Maybe the lady who did the scan measured wrong, I really didn't know. What I did know though was that this letter confirmed our baby was viable, which in my mind always had been.

I continued going to work, during quiet moments my mind would always focus on the tiny little human I was growing inside of me. This pregnancy was consuming all my thoughts. I would always be rubbing my belly and declaring my absolute love every moment my attention was drawn to it. I didn't even look pregnant I hardly had a bump. I always thought people got their bumps within weeks of finding out. You would have never known I was expecting unless I'd told you. However I did look unwell. I was suffering terribly with sickness and I was also anemic.

I was at work one day and came over feeling really unwell, it was a sudden feeling. I went to sit in the back office of the store and from nowhere I was sick, all over the desk. I had to go home and rest, my colleagues could see I wasn't right and they all told me to go and look after myself and my baby, it was the most important thing at that time. I contacted the doctor and was signed off from work until I could start maternity leave. I was upset because once again things were going very differently for me, unlike every other pregnant person I just wasn't well enough to carry on as normal.

Was I doing something wrong or was I just not handling things like other people who are pregnant? Was the sickness and feelings of being unwell completely normal? I really didn't want to let work down. I had a great job and I didn't want to jeopardise it in any way. I'd built up a reputation of being very reliable, I would rarely take a day off from work, so this situation was deeply upsetting in many ways. I would spend most of my days getting plenty of bedrest, it gave me lots of time to bond with my tiny bump and I knew that ultimately everything would be worth it.

When the twenty-week scan came round I was again full of excitement. Since I had received the letter I had completely dismissed the possibility that anything could be wrong. We were going to be seeing our baby again, that was all that mattered to me. At that time of this pregnancy they didn't tell you the gender of the baby, but whichever it was, it was already deeply loved and cherished.

We were once again sitting in the waiting room of the very busy maternity department. Once again after a wait we were called and went in for the scan. I lay down on the bed and lifted my top up to reveal my tiny precious little bump. Very cold gel was applied for the scan. My eyes then fixed on the monitor, eagerly awaiting a glimpse of our little baby. I saw flutters of movement on the screen and my heart swelled with love. The baby's heartbeat was again very strong, but this time the baby wasn't measuring right. The sonographer looked very concerned and left the room. After twenty or so minutes she returned, asking me to come back the following day so a consultant could perform the scan. We left, both were feeling very confused and me extremely upset.

When we got home, Jack went back to work and I broke down on the floor crying my heart out, "please be ok baby, I love you so much!!". I was feeling very sick, my head was throbbing and my eyes were swollen from all of the crying. This was so scary. I needed that time on my own to try and digest the information. It is very worrying when you know something is wrong and you're in that limbo period of not knowing what it is. I just couldn't switch my mind off from this really scary reality. I hadn't known anyone else who had encountered the same scenario as this one I was now experiencing.

After the longest twenty-four-hours we went back to the hospital. Sitting in the waiting room with all the happy couples was so hard, it did not feel the same for me now. I was not excited just absolutely terrified. I didn't want the pain I was experiencing to show, if I did it may have spoilt the scan experience that the other couples in the room were having. I was trying to remain calm and keep a strong positive mindset.

We were waiting for long over an hour, I then heard my name called out and we were asked to go into a different room to where we had previously been seen. A consultant introduced himself and was ready to do the scan. I got myself on to the bed and my eyes, once again, fixated onto the screen. The consultant wasn't talking but he was spending a lengthy amount of time doing the scan. He turned to me and Jack and said, "I have seen this before, just last year and your baby will be absolutely fine, it's just measuring small with the limbs. Your baby has achondroplasia, which is a form of dwarfism. They will lead a perfectly normal life; however, they will only reach a height of around four feet". The baby last year has been born and was doing really well. It was all very reassuring to hear, I was so relieved our baby was okay. I hadn't ever heard of the word achondroplasia so of course I spent a lot of time researching and learning about it to better prepare myself for what was to come. I was already deeply in love with our precious gift who was growing inside of me, nothing could change that and I was prepared to do anything.

It was fairly easy after that to get our head around the diagnosis our baby had been given, both myself and Jack, once again, became excited. We would talk about how cute our baby would be and how all good things come in small packages.

I had an antenatal appointment six weeks later and asked my mum to come along with me, as Jack was working. It was a nice day, the sun was shining and I drove and picked mum up. Off we went to the maternity department of the hospital. I was getting mild stomach cramps but being a first-time mum, I put the uncomfortable feelings down to, what I thought were, normal side effects of the pregnancy. All of the standard checks from a routine antenatal appointment were fine and we left. I spent the day with mum and we stayed out and grabbed some lunch together. We had a few lovely hours. I dropped her off at her house about 5pm and drove home to be with Jack.

When I got there, Jacks dad was in the kitchen, he looked at me and said, "she doesn't look right". I hadn't noticed but throughout the day the cramping pains had been getting worse and I was leaning against the work top. "I am fine", I said, "it's just growing pains from the baby, I've been getting them on and off for a while". He then said to Jack, "she's not fine, that is not normal at all, call an ambulance". That completely threw me, was I getting all this wrong, yet again? I was checked just that morning I knew I was fine. It was the 18th February, 2008. I was twenty-six weeks and six days pregnant. The ambulance came and said they were going to take me in just to be checked over, "it's more than likely Braxton hicks, you'll be fine we're just being precautionary".

It was now dark and very foggy, I was taken to the biggest hospital in the area and given gas and air. The cramps were becoming stronger. It felt like the baby was dropping. I had no idea what was going on and before I knew it I was in a room being examined. I heard a voice say "this baby isn't waiting, we're going to give you a dose of steroids to help the baby's lungs as you're so early". Before long there must have been twenty people in the room and a metal trolley had been brought in. My baby wasn't ready though, I couldn't be giving birth now, it wasn't right. The baby wasn't due until May 19th, it was too early, I was so incredibly scared.

"Don't worry, babies are born prematurely all the time and most do really well". The pain was increasing, I was feeling increasingly traumatised, there was so much going on around me and so many eyes were on me. They were desperately trying to get our baby out, it was showing signs of distress. I just couldn't do it, I didn't even know what to do. I had a cannula inserted and was about to sign the form for an emergency c-section. As I did, I had the urge to give one hard push and with that my baby was born. Everything was very quiet, there was not a single sound. Our baby was quickly picked up, put on to the trolley and rushed out of the room. It all happened in seconds, I still didn't know what was going on.

To me one minute I was pregnant going about my day and the next thing I had just gone through a traumatic birthing experience. I did not even know if my baby was alive, I didn't hear a cry, I didn't know what gender it was, I didn't know anything. Physically, as soon as I had given birth the feelings of being unwell quickly subsided, but my mind was now in turmoil. Two hours after the birth, a nurse came in to me, "we have managed to stabilise her and she is doing okay now, we almost lost her, everyone is doing the very best they can for your daughter". In that one moment I had found out I had a daughter and my daughter had almost died. I cannot explain to you how that felt, I was in what I can only describe as an autopilot state of mind. Nothing felt real, it was like the worst bad dream I had ever had, but it was all real, it wasn't a dream at all.

I turned to the nurse and asked, "can I see her?". "No, not yet we are still working on her and I'm going to take you up to the maternity ward, you will be in your own room so away from the other mothers and babies, someone will come and get you and you can meet your baby girl. We need to have her transferred to a hospital with a higher-level neonatal unit, we'll keep you updated on that".

My mum had come to the hospital, she had been waiting in the corridor for news. Jack had been backwards and forwards keeping her updated. I was told the maternity ward was ready for me. Mum and Jack left and I went to my private room on the maternity ward. I lay on the bed and cried my heart out over what had just happened. I felt completely alone again, I needed Jack and my baby with me. I went to the hospital completely unprepared because I did not expect to be giving birth, I had no hospital bag, no clean clothes, no toiletries. Jack came back with a bag of things for me and a set of pyjamas, he quickly left again though, it must have been the early hours of the morning by now. I got changed, still in this autopilot state of mind, the feelings of everything I had experienced didn't feel real. I again lay in the bed in a complete daze, I kept rubbing my belly but my baby wasn't there anymore. I could not rest or sleep. I felt more alone than I had ever felt before in my entire life. I had definitely never been more traumatised than I was now.

I wanted to meet my baby so badly and just to be there for her. I still hadn't seen her yet and was desperately waiting for someone to come and get me so I could go into the special care baby unit. At 4am someone did come to get me, I sat in a wheelchair and was taken to her. There was an incubator with so many wires and transfusions going into it, the monitor was showing good stats. Inside the incubator was this tiny but very beautiful baby girl. I can't explain in words how much love I felt. I couldn't see her face properly as she was on a ventilator. I told her I was so sorry, she should still be inside of me instead of in this vulnerable state, being kept alive with machinery and drugs. She should still be in me, with me keeping her alive, not all of this. What on earth had I done, why didn't I stop this from happening?

She didn't look like she had short limbs, she was the most beautiful little thing I had ever seen. Her skin was dark pink, she was so underdeveloped. She really wasn't ready for the world yet and neither was I ready for her. Her tiny little cheeks were so bruised from the birth, I couldn't imagine how she was feeling or the pain she might be in. I put my hand inside the incubator to hold her tiny little hand and she gripped my pinky so tightly. “Mummy’s here now, I’ll be so strong for you I promise, hello my beautiful baby girl, my Imogen Lily”. I couldn’t take my eyes off from her, I was mesmerized. It felt like I had been thrusted into another world which I had never known before or even knew existed, just a few hours ago she was a flutter in my belly.

A nurse came and told me there was a neonatal ambulance on its way to transfer Imogen. They were going to be taking her to the Royal London hospital in Whitechapel, London. I had to go back to the room on the maternity ward as they needed to work with Imogen and have her ready for the transfer. I was told I would be updated and would get the chance to see her before she went. I went back to my room feeling a little calmer and confident, knowing that she was in good hands. I was feeling absolutely exhausted so when I lay my head down, I managed to get a few hours' sleep.

Chapter 8: 174 Days

February 2008

I woke up and for a split moment I had completely forgotten about what had happened, then as soon as I opened my eyes I realised. I was lying in a hospital bed in a side room to the maternity ward. I rubbed my belly like I had been doing so often, only now it felt completely different. It was empty, my baby wasn't there but she wasn't with me either, there wasn't a tiny cot next to me. My baby was downstairs in the special care baby unit. A nurse came and offered me something to eat but I didn't have an appetite, I just wanted to go and see my beautiful baby girl. The nurse then said, "Imogen was transferred at 6am, she is now at the hospital in London". How had she gone? I was told I would be able to see her before she left, I needed to go and go right now. "Discharge me please". I phoned Jack, told him what was going on and that he needed to come and pick me up as soon as possible and that I'd be waiting at the front of the hospital for him.

They discharged me because they understood the urgency of me needing to go. I went outside to wait for Jack, it took him three hours to get to me. It was a freezing February day, I had just given birth, extremely prematurely, our baby was in a critical condition in London and it took him three hours! What on earth could have been more important to do than this? I was in a terrible state. As soon as I got into the car I said to Jack, "where were you? We need to go and we need to go now!!". He hadn't packed anything for us so we had to go back to the flat to quickly grab what we thought we would need before we make the drive over to the hospital. By now time was really pressing on and the hospital was seventy miles away.

When we arrived at the Royal London hospital I frantically ran to the front desk, "I need to go to the Elizabeth ward, my baby was transferred here through the night". We were directed to the ward and we made our way as quickly as possible. We headed straight to the desk on the ward, "we're Imogen Lily's parents". "Why has it taken you so long to get here? We have had to bag her twice!". In other words she had stopped breathing twice since she had arrived. "We've got her stabilised for the moment, come with me and I'll take you to her".

As we went in the room all we could see were incubators, there must have been at least thirty. There were tiny beautiful little babies inside each and every one, Imogen was to the left-hand side of the room and in the third incubator along. There were monitors constantly sounding off, transfusions linked to almost every baby. It was a very sad sight to see, not a world that I had ever known or seen before. This would be the first time Jack would see his daughter. I felt utterly useless, I couldn't even make a baby right. I really didn't know how he was feeling, but he must have felt so scared.

Imogen was currently stable and looked as though she was just sleeping, she was still on the life support. We sat with her for as long as we could. Then realisation kicked in, where were we going to sleep tonight? I didn't want to go home and leave her. What on earth would we do? We went to the desk and asked for help. Because I had just given birth, I would be able to spend a night on the maternity ward, but Jack couldn't. When we got to the maternity ward I broke down, I begged them to let Jack stay with me which they allowed, for just one night. We were given a private room and told that Jack must not be seen by any of the other women on the ward.

The maternity ward got in touch with the Sick Children's Trust charity for us. They have houses where parents can stay if they have children in the hospital and run solely on donations. They provided us with a room, we were beyond grateful to them. We had somewhere to stay whilst Imogen was in London, it was such a massive relief, one that we will always be grateful for.

Jack was given two weeks off from his employer and my maternity leave from work began. We could fully concentrate on being with Imogen. I went and bought her the tiniest nappies I could find, some baby wipes and all the usual baby bits. I had to express milk which was fed to her by a tube. That in itself was another awful experience, it just didn't feel natural and I developed an emotional and mental block to expressing, it broke my heart. I would wash her with cotton wool and sterilised water and did everything else I was able to do but I couldn't hold her, I wasn't allowed too yet. I longed for the time when I could just pick her up and hold her close in my arms where she was meant to be. She was alive and she was improving, the time for cuddles would one day come and when it did, I would never ever let her go.

Imogen was growing rapidly and I would spend most of every day sitting on a chair next to her, my hand inside the incubator just holding on to her and letting her know I was there. Jack had to go back to work after two weeks and I found myself there with no one else. It was just me and Imogen. She was slowly but surely improving but there were many setbacks throughout the days. It was a long while before she came of life support and was moved on to the c-pap, which helps with breathing and keeps the oxygen levels up. Her stats were consistently good, the signs of her being okay her positive.

One day I'd gone into the ward and was stopped by the consultant, he requested a meeting. "Imogen's lungs are not developing normally, there is a lot we know but also a lot we don't know, this falls into the don't know". He showed me an x-ray of her lungs in comparison to a normal set of lungs. Imogen's rib cage was growing at a slower rate than her lungs, meaning there wasn't enough space for her lungs. This was so hard to hear, how could this be when she was showing only positive signs of progression. I left the meeting and went back to be with her, silently crying. I could feel the tears rolling down my cheeks. This was a lot for one person to handle. Jack was only coming up at the weekend's, sometimes on a Friday and staying for two nights, but mostly coming on a Saturday and staying just the one night. He didn't seem understand the seriousness of the situation, either that or he was just doing his best to block it all out.

During his time away from me he had been messaging other women, giving them a sob story about how hard his life was at the moment, he was pretty much fishing for sympathy. What he wouldn't say is he was barely dealing with it at all and was leaving everything to me. In all honesty he was hardly any support at all. It was almost guaranteed that before he would leave us to go home, he would ask me for money. The reason he wasn't with us was because he was working, did he really need to take the money I had from me?

It was during this time I thought back to my own childhood, how my life was and how I was treated. When I looked at my baby girl all I felt was pure love. How on earth could anyone hurt a child they brought into the world? All the hurt and pain I felt towards those who had hurt me some simply diminished. None of it mattered any more. What mattered to me was this tiny little human that I had created, she was the most important thing in the world. Everything I would do from now on would be for the greater good of my Imogen. Her just being there healed me from my past and gave me a fresh perspective on life. My life mattered now because her life mattered. I wasn't on this earth to fix anybody, and I certainly wasn't going to tolerate anyone doing any wrong to me or her anymore. Jack had let us both down on so many levels. The love towards him that I had felt for all those years was fading away. I felt sorry for him but he was old enough to take responsibility for his own life and I was sick and tired of feeling the way I did because of him. If my life was only going to have me and Imogen in it, then so be it.

I was called for another meeting with the consultant, Imogen's eyes were not developing normally due to her severe prematurity. She needed laser eye surgery to save her tunnel vision sight, but she would forever lose her peripheral vision. She would also need to be fully sedated for the treatment to be carried out. I was absolutely terrified for her. Would she even survive the sedation, would she ever wake up again? She depended on so much to be alive yet it was vital she had the eye surgery and it couldn't wait. I phoned Jack but he did not seem to care enough to come and be with us. Whatever he had going on at home was far more important. I sat with Imogen until the very last moment when they wheeled her incubator out the ward and took her off to be sedated.

My mind was running at a thousand miles an hour. I was completely on my own feeling petrified that my baby would never wake up again. I left the children's department, sat on a bench outside of the building and cried my heart out. I was so scared for my daughter, my absolute world, my everything. Another mum who also had a baby on the same ward saw me crying, she didn't say a word, just sat down beside me and gave me the biggest hug. That set me off even more. I managed to calm myself enough to tell her what was happening and she stayed with me until I had the call to say that Imogen had come round and was back on the ward. The surgery had thankfully been successful.

Imogen was now four months old, or one month according to her original due date. The Royal London teamed up with Great Ormand Street hospital to examine her, Imogen's diagnosis of achondroplasia was not fitting with her symptoms. She had a full body x-ray and I was able to stay with her throughout, to put her into the positions she needed to be in for it. I thought nothing more of it until three weeks later when the consultant, once again, requested a meeting. This time he stressed that he wanted Jack present and stated it was urgent.

I called Jack and he said he would be with me as soon as he could be, but days passed, and he still didn't come. The consultant once again stopped me in the ward and explained that what he had to say really could not wait. I had to have the meeting on my own, without Jack who clearly had more important things to do. The consultant said, "I am sorry, but Imogen's diagnosis of achondroplasia is not correct. Imogen has achondrogenesis type two, which is a fatal condition, sadly we need to put Imogen onto palliative care. Babies born with achondrogenesis pass away within hours of birth, in all honesty it's a miracle she is still with us".

My world in that one moment completely shattered. I went straight to Imogen, tears uncontrollably streaming down my face, struggling to contemplate the fact that I had to begin the process of letting her go, my baby was going to die. Everything I had been told regarding her condition was wrong, she was never going to be okay. I had sat by her side for five months, mostly on my own, caring for her. The love I had for her was so very deep, she was my everything and I had to let her go. My beautiful first-born child, my precious baby girl.

I think throughout all that time at the hospital I had remained on auto pilot. I don't know how I would have coped if I had processed everything as it had happened. I'd had to be so strong. I had to have the strength to get up and dressed every day, to go and be with her, to be her mum.

With the palliative care came her deterioration. Her stats started dropping each day, her oxygen levels becoming dangerously low. Every day was one closer to losing her. I couldn't face being anywhere else but by her side. No one and nothing were more important than Imogen. She had the most beautiful big blue eyes and I'm sure she was smiling at me with them throughout our time together. I cherished every single moment we had. I'd only been able to hold her in my arms once, which was when she came off the ventilator and on to the c-pap. None of this was fair.

On the 9th August, 2008, I went to the ward and was told it was time to turn the machines off and let her go. I can't explain how gut wrenching it was to hear those words. She was no longer on the neonatal ward but in the special care baby unit, in a big girls cot. Jack had come over and we were saying goodbye to our baby girl. In my mind I was saying to her, "don't go Imogen, they have been wrong up to now, prove them all wrong again, please baby girl, don't go, please don't leave me, I love you so very much". I knew she couldn't hear my thoughts, no one could, but those were the kind of thoughts I was having at the time.

She was taken off the machines she had needed, all the wires on her tiny little body were gone, the life support was removed from her beautiful tiny little face. It was the first time I got to properly hold my daughter, the first time I got to see her, without the stuff which had been keeping her here with me. I couldn't let her go, but I had too, she had suffered so much in her short life. It wouldn't be fair to let her suffer any more though she wasn't in any pain.

I was holding her for a while, constantly looking around at the nurses and consultants surrounding us. She wasn't going anywhere. After four hours they made the decision to put her back on the aids she needed. She wasn't going to die, not today. That's my girl, strong like her mum.

The next day we went to the ward and her stats were better than they had been for weeks, they had been wrong I knew it! I made comments to the nurses about how well she was doing, they were all in agreement with me, then the consultant came and shattered any hope once again. "She wasn't ready to go when we tried yesterday, we're going to try again tomorrow". I was mentally, physically and emotionally drained, I really didn't know how much more I could take. I was away from my life, home, everyone I knew. There were very few people that made the journey over to be there for me and meet Imogen. People said they cared, but did they really? I had built up so many negative emotions towards everyone I knew, I felt incredibly let down. The truth is that no one was really there for us, except for Marley, she was the exception. Marley had offered on several occasions to come and be with me but she was pregnant herself and I didn't want her to see any of this in her condition.

All of this happened before social media platforms had taken off, so I didn't even have that to help get me through.

I dressed Imogen in a little white dress with pink lining, it wasn't the prettiest dress but because she was so small not a lot else fit her. She was being sick a lot and her eyes were starting to bulge. She really couldn't take much more and if the truth be told, I could see that. I was wishing with everything I had for a miracle but that was never going to be. She didn't deserve any of this. She was a pure soul, a new little life that only knew the noise of monitors constantly beeping and people walking by her but barely stopping to look in on her. In six short months she had shown and taught me so much about life. She fought desperately each and every day to survive, it was all just too much to take. We had some photos taken by one of the nurses, our first family photo and a beautiful photo of Imogen.

The following day we went up to the ward, things were as normal as normal was for us now. I was looking after Imogen whilst she lay in her cot, changing her when she needed it, washing her with the cotton wool and water. Singing to her whilst stroking her head and holding her tiny little hand. Then at 4pm I heard someone behind me say, "we're going to try again now, we really need to let Imogen go".

My mind screamed No! I can't do this, I can't watch my baby die! All the thoughts I was having were silent though. To the other people around me in the same room I just wasn't talking. They didn't know the pure torture that was going on inside my head. I was taken to the same chair I had sat in two days earlier and the curtain drawn around us. Imogen was again disconnected from what was keeping her alive. This time it felt so different. She was showing obvious signs of letting go. After an hour I placed her back in the cot seeing her fast deterioration before my eyes, tears again streaming, I started to have a panic attack, this was real. I said out loud, so everyone heard me, "I can't do this, I can't watch her die!!". I ran out of the ward and out of the hospital, struggling to catch my breath. It was the most difficult pain I had ever experienced in my life. Nothing compares to the pain of having to go through what I did then. I tried so hard to calm myself down, Imogen needed me.

My phone rang, "you need to get back here... NOW!". I ran as fast as I could, back through the hospital, back to the Elizabeth ward. "She's almost gone". I sat back down and Imogen was placed in my arms for the very last time. In my mind I told her to go, but to make sure she comes back to me, in a healthy body. "I love you so, so much". I placed my hand gently on her chest, it was barely moving at all. I felt the reduced rate of her breathing, there was no monitor anymore so I had no idea of what her stats were. Very soon after, as I cradled Imogen in my arms, it was declared, "she is gone, time of death 11:56 pm".

My heart shattered in to a million pieces, I was holding her so close that my tears were falling onto her peaceful beautiful little face. She had left me, she had just died in my arms. Imogen wasn't suffering anymore, but my mind was racing. Why her? Why MY baby? She did nothing to deserve this. What had I done to deserve all the heartache I had endured throughout my life and now the greatest pain of them all. I kissed Imogen's forehead, "make sure you come back to me Imogen, next time in a healthy body, I love you so much baby girl".

It was also the anniversary of Jack's brother's death. "He must have come and got her", he said. We were both completely broken, but the night wasn't over. I placed Imogen back into her cot and I was told to get her washed and changed. I had to remove her clothes from her tiny lifeless body, the nurse took prints of her hands and feet, then I washed her. I had to change her nappy, and then dress her into the outfit that would remain on her forever. I couldn't bear the thought of her cold and alone, so I chose to dress her for the last time in a warm tracksuit. The whole process took time, but it was extra moments with her I wasn't expecting, I never knew these were things that had to be done. I lay her in a woven basket cot, gave her another kiss and watched her be taken away to the mortuary. We left the ward with the few belongings Imogen had and the prints of her hands and feet. I had never felt so completely heartbroken as I felt right then in that moment of time.

Back at the room in the Sick Children's Trust house, I lay on the bed still fully clothed, feeling utterly drained and completely broken hearted. I lay there with tears flowing, my worst nightmare had been realised, so many thoughts flooded my mind. I was speechless and silent, but my mind was louder than ever. I was screaming inside and feeling the deepest pain I had ever felt in my entire life. It wasn't a physical pain, but mentally crippling. How could I ever be alright when my beautiful girl had not long since taken her last breath? How would I ever smile again?

I wouldn't ever be happy, my life never had been, what did I do that was so wrong to deserve this complete and utter heartbreak? Why did she have to leave me? Why was it my baby that had to go through all of this? Why couldn't things have been different? Why couldn't she have had a healthy body? My mind just wouldn't stop, between all of these questions were the mental images of what I'd seen. The images of her passing, the sensations of touching her lifeless little body, the smell of her, the twinkling look in her beautiful eyes as they closed for the final time. I had absolutely no control over the thoughts, I just couldn't stop them. For the last 174 days, which is almost six months, after getting ready for the day I had headed straight to the hospital to be with Imogen and be the best mum I could be to her.

My world then quite simply stopped. We had known that she was going to die, but until it happened, I'd always held on to a little bit of hope. With Imogen now gone it was so much worse than I had ever imagined it would be.

I rang the mortuary and asked if I could see Imogen, I was desperate to see her and be her mum. I thought I could go there whenever I wanted as I had done when she was in the ward, but the mortuary doesn't work that way. They gave me an appointment time of 2pm. I also had to register her death at Bow registry office as she had died in their borough, an appointment was made there for 10am the following morning.

We had to pack up our belongings from the Sick Children's Trust, it had been 'home' for six months but so many people need their rooms. I was still seeing familiar faces there whose worlds were the same as ours but who were still able to be with their children. I couldn't face speaking to anyone.

2pm finally came and I was able to see Imogen. I still had a vision in my mind from when I last saw her and wasn't mentally prepared or aware of what I was about to walk into. As I went in I saw her beautiful angelic face, she looked like she was peacefully asleep. There wasn't a sound to be heard. I asked if I could hold her and carefully picked her up from the basket, I couldn't bear the thought of not holding her again. She was my baby and I'd missed out on so many cuddles, this one was to be the last. She was so cold and there was no movement at all, I can only describe it as holding a cold porcelain doll. My heart broke again, I hadn't thought that I wouldn't ever again feel the warmth of her perfect skin or her squidgy little cheeks again, she was completely frozen. I stroked her beautiful face, taking in as much as I could. There were features of her face I had barely seen before because she had always had breathing aids covering her. I told her over and over again how much I loved her. I had learnt so much about life through her and how I wished things had been different. I lay her back down and gave her a final kiss goodbye. That was the last time I ever lay eyes on my beautiful baby girl, my Imogen Lily.

I never stopped crying, my head hurt so badly, my mind would just not go quiet. I felt so much hatred towards so many people who had made such little effort through the hardest time in my life. All those people who never gave a thought to come and meet my daughter whilst they had the chance too.

We would be going home the next morning so we loaded the car and then went to bed, I can't say I slept much, how could I? Even with feeling as drained as I did, I just couldn't switch off, haunted by the fact my baby was lying across the road in a freezer.

After getting up and ready the next morning we gave the room a final clean, stripped the beds and made sure we had all of our belongings. I had a car full of baby stuff and paperwork, but no baby to take home with me. We still had to register her death and walked from the Royal London hospital to Bow registry office. Nothing seemed very real and it didn't seem to take very long, we were straight in to do what we had to do.

The lady was very nice but I could see it was hard for her to register the death and then there I had it in my hand, the death certificate.

We walked back to the hospital and to the Elizabeth ward to give our thanks for everything they had all done for Imogen. We walked back to the Sick Children's Trust and gave thanks to them. It was important to do that because without those people, our lives would have been so much harder. I'd had six months with Imogen and I'd been able to completely focus on her without the worry about where I was going to sleep. The car was parked outside the mortuary where we were leaving our beautiful daughter behind, that made me feel physically sick. As we drove away, I kept my eyes on the building until it couldn't be seen anymore. Goodbye my darling, I love you so, so much.

Chapter 9: The Aftermath

August 2008

On the way home from London, Jack told me we, technically, didn't have a home to go back to. What I hadn't known was that Jack was in trouble with his job, he had sold my car and he had also lost our home. Our baby had just died and I didn't even have my own home to go back too. Could things have got any worse than this? All I wanted was to go home and get in my bed, that I hadn't seen in six months, and have a bit of time alone to reflect and grieve. I had really had enough of him by now, how much did one person have to take? Everything completely tipped me over the edge and all I wanted was to be with Imogen.

I phoned my mum and explained the situation to her and she told me to go back to hers. I said to Jack, "I can't deal with anything else, please just leave me alone, you were barely there for me and Imogen, now you're telling me all this, I just cannot do it anymore, I have nothing left in me to give". I had absolutely no idea how he was feeling, our relationship had always been up and down but this situation had put so much more stress on the both of us, it completely broke us apart. I went back to mums but couldn't face anyone or anything.

Jack didn't leave me alone like I had asked him too, he hounded me, threatening his life if I wasn't with him. He couldn't see all the damage he had done. I knew he was grieving too but he left me and Imogen because of his job and our flat. What was it all for? We didn't have the flat and I hadn't got a car, which I greatly depended on.

We still had the funeral to arrange and we had to do that together. After much persistence and him using my grief against me, saying his family thought I wasn't being fair and that I was acting completely in the wrong and with the threats to his own life, I agreed to go back to him and for us to find somewhere else to live. We found a little cottage which had fairly cheap rent, it seemed ideal. I bought a little Fiesta, so I had a car again and we had everything in place for Imogen's funeral. With everything else I couldn't afford to pay for the funeral in one go and the funeral director kindly let me pay in monthly instalments. I had never managed to save any money and I had never imagined I would have the expense of a funeral to pay for at just twenty-four years old.

Imogen was collected from London by the funeral directors, we had arranged for a family plot near Jack's other family members. We were as ready as we would ever be to lay our daughter to rest. The funeral was held on the 5th September. We made our way to mum's house as it was previously arranged the funeral would start from there. A single black Mercedes limousine pulled up outside. On the middle row of seats was Imogen in her tiny white coffin. It was the closest she had ever been to home. I got into the car and it slowly made its journey to the small church within the cemetery grounds. Jack carried her little coffin and I walked along beside him. All I could hear were the cries of the people waiting inside the church.

As I was standing listening to the service my legs began trembling like nothing I had ever experienced before, I have never experienced anything like it since. I could barely stand from all the emotion that was running through me. Quite a few people turned up but I couldn't get my head around how they hadn't turned up to the hospital to show their support and love there. It was a short service, I wasn't interested in hearing about God. I wondered again if God was real then why did all this suffering happening. My mind had been made up over God since I was a child. Imogen's tiny coffin was carried out of the church and down to her forever resting place. At her plot there was a small, but very deep hole, it was right where the headstone would be. I thought that was nice because at least I knew no one would be walking over her. With a few words being said she was slowly lowered into the ground. As I looked down I threw a flower on to her coffin. I just wanted to pull her back up and keep her forever, but she was gone and was never coming back. "Rest in peace my beautiful baby girl, I hope one day we will meet again".

Slowly one by one people left the service, not really knowing what to say to me, so instead embracing me with a hug and saying how sorry they were. There were a lot of flowers with little cards of sympathy. I stayed with Imogen as long as I could, I wanted to keep the mental image of what I was seeing as a firm memory in my mind. We made our way to the wake but I couldn't bear it, people were happily talking amongst themselves and I really wasn't in the mood for talking or socialising with anyone. In all honesty I can't even remember who was or wasn't there. I left with Jack, it was all far too much. We just wanted to be left alone. None of those people knew her and I just couldn't do it, it all seemed very false.

After the funeral things were very hard, I was suffering with such deep grief. A few weeks had passed and I hadn't yet been able to face going to the cemetery. I knew it needed sorting out as the flowers from the funeral would need clearing. I drove over to mum in the hope she could help me and on the way I stopped at a supermarket to buy a small bunch of flowers. When I got to mum's house I went in and she offered me a cup of tea. Whilst we were sitting there I said that I needed to go to the cemetery and asked her for her help. She looked me square in the eyes and said, "I don't do graves, do it yourself'. I felt like a dagger had just pierced my heart, I was speechless not believing how she had just responded to my request of help. I put my cup of tea on the table and walked out. I was so upset, my daughter had just died yet she didn't have a care for her own daughter. It just felt so cruel. I drove to the cemetery alone with my small bouquet. When I got there all the flowers were indeed dead, the white flowers had turned brown, it was an awful mess. I knelt down on the wet grass and started to clear it up and put it all in the bin nearby. All that was left was a wooden cross with her name and the date which she passed away on and the few fresh flowers I had brought with me. I sat there on the wet grass for ages, just sobbing. It became my little place to escape too, whenever things were bad and I needed to get out, I went to Imogen. It always saddened me that I couldn't afford a headstone but the funeral had to be paid off, in full, before I could even think about that which just broke my heart even more, she deserved it all and I couldn't afford to give it her.

Jack still wasn't working, and my maternity leave was only a few weeks from being reduced to statuary pay. I had to turn my attention onto going back to work. A new branch was opening in a nearby town and I requested a transfer which was accepted. I went in to help get the new store ready and it wasn't long before I was behind the counter dealing with customers again.

One customer came in very upset over a rather trivial matter of course he didn't know what I had just been through and if he had, maybe he would have been kinder. I walked away from said customer and asked my manager to take over.

Other than the fact that work was a great distraction, it brought a little bit of normality back in my life. What was hard was going home to Jack who did nothing but play computer games all day, he wasn't proactively looking for a new job and was completely dependent on me. I couldn't afford to keep going the way I was, I had gone back to work on a part time basis as it was all I could mentally cope with at that time.

I still had healing to do within myself, it was going to take me a long time to heal from all the pain. I brought the matter up with Jack several times and one day he just lost it with me. He told me to get off his back and that all I did was moan. He told me I was a mess, a state, that he didn't know why he was with me. He kept calling me Annie, short for Annie-rexic. I barely had any weight to me, but the mental pain had also turned physical, I wasn't eating a lot at all. I needed looking after, just for once in my life. I had always had to look after myself and other people. I just wanted someone, anyone, to look after me this time.

I went to the doctor and he diagnosed me with anxiety and depression, I refused to be signed off because I couldn't afford to not work. He gave me antidepressants, which I didn't want so I didn't take, and sleeping tablets. I had told him I was struggling to sleep, which I was. I just wanted to block everything and everyone out and sleep.

Jack started on me once again telling me I was pathetic and embarrassed him. When I had asked him if he had any luck in finding another job, he held me up against the wall telling me to back off and shut up about it, screaming the words and spitting in my face. Whilst still having a hold of me he forcefully threw me across the room and I fell to the floor. "I ain't putting up with this I'm going out". With that Jack stormed out and I ran upstairs.

I couldn't take it anymore, I wanted it to stop, "MAKE IT ALL STOP!" I reached for the sleeping tablets and poured a few out onto my hand, not enough to do any damage, but enough to ensure they would work. I put them all in my mouth and washed them down with the glass of water which was on the table beside the bed. I could rest now, I just wanted to rest, for my mind to just stop. I didn't want to hurt anymore, I just need a break. I lay down on the bed, in a surprisingly relatively calm state. I didn't want to die, I just wanted to rest. I wanted quiet surroundings and a quiet mind. I slowly drifted off into a very deep sleep.

When I woke up it was early evening, I had slept the day away. I could hear the TV, Jack was downstairs and I slowly made my way down, not knowing what his reception to me would be like. I still felt very drained, mentally and physically. The grief I was experiencing was extremely intense. "I am sorry", he said. "You know I don't mean to get like that, it's just hard you know, you going on at me all the time really doesn't help". I didn't have the energy to get into anything else with him. "I know Jack, I'm sorry too, it isn't our fault things are like they are, we've just been really unlucky, things will get better".

A few days later I noticed I was feeling more tired than usual. Jack looked at me and said "I think you're pregnant". I hadn't even thought that I could be, it had taken months to fall pregnant with Imogen. I wasn't feeling anything like I had when I was pregnant with her. Although I didn't believe that I was pregnant, I still asked Jack if he could go and buy a pregnancy test. He did, he wasn't gone long and handed it to me. "You better go and do it now". With that I went to the bathroom, did the test and put it back in the box without waiting for the result. "Well?" said Jack. "I don't know, I haven't looked, it takes two minutes". We' both sat at the kitchen table with the box between us, I picked the box up, took the test out and looked at the result. "It's positive, I am pregnant". With that, we just looked at each other with a scared look. What if it all happens again? How are we going to get through this again? I do hope everything is better this time around.

It was now December and I hadn't been back at work long, we had only lost Imogen four months prior. I was still in an extremely delicate state. It wasn't at all as exciting as the first time. I was so scared and anxious. I didn't even know deep down if I wanted to be with Jack, but what I did want was for Imogen to come back to me, she could only do that if it was the same parents. I know it sounds crazy, but grief does strange things to your mind.

I was physically feeling much better with this pregnancy, I didn't need to take time off from work. The first scan came and I was so nervous because this is where we had the first clue something was wrong last time. I lay there whilst the scan was being performed, nervously waiting to hear what she's thinking regarding the pregnancy. "All is looking very good; everything is measuring correctly". I sighed the biggest sigh of relief; it was only a year ago that things had been so very different. We were given a due date for the 8th August and given a photo of the scan. I left feeling so much better, but the weight wasn't lifted, I wasn't going to feel fully relaxed and content until this baby was safely in my arms.

Although I had a constant worry in the back of my mind, the pregnancy progressed well. I was still coming to terms with what had happened with Imogen though and was trying to handle the grieving process as best as I could. I was alright one minute and the next my mind would be flooded with thoughts.

Then in February 2009 a letter came through the post. It was a letter from Belgium where samples from Imogen had been sent off for analysis to confirm her diagnosis. The bottom line of it was that no abnormalities were found within Imogen, everything was showing as normal and she had neither condition she was diagnosed with. I struggled to comprehend what I was reading. Ever since I received this letter I can't help but think that maybe she would be with me today if she hadn't received the care according to the diagnosis she was given. I will never know what was truly wrong and why she died. It was all very confusing, like when they had told me about her lungs, I couldn't make sense of that either. I am aware that the ventilator caused chronic lung disease as she was on it for so long, but that was done according to the achondroplasia diagnosis. We had been offered genetics testing but I was so done with everything I turned it down, I couldn't cope with anymore and not only that, but I was also already pregnant again. It was really already too late.

With the pregnancy Jack upped his game in finding a job, he managed to get one with a large online car auction company as a yard supervisor. It was just what we both needed and I really hoped again that things would get better. We felt we could start buying what we needed for the baby with the hope that this time we would be using them, we hadn't bought much last time around, besides a few clothes. We were given a cot and bought a Moses basket, pram, car seat, bottles, nappies and everything else we thought we would need.

Mum out of the blue contacted me saying she was emigrating to Geneva for work, I was slightly shocked, it was a long way to go but she was set on it. I'm sure she had always resented her life and took the first opportunity she was given to stop being a mum. Charlotte was now at university, Tom and Josh had moved out. I asked her what was happening with the house she was still renting; she had been living there for eight years now. She suggested I got in touch with the landlord. Her house was bigger and more suitable for a family than the small cottage we were living in. I contacted her landlord to let him know that mum was planning on leaving and requested to take over the tenancy. He agreed straightaway. It was all timed perfectly as our six-month tenancy was due for renewal.

We didn't have much to do because we didn't have much and we hadn't lived in the cottage long, however, we had a lot to do in mum's house. She pretty much just took what she wanted and left the rest for us to sort out. I could have done without that in my condition, but it would be worth it so we just got on with it.

We moved in. She had left a few items of furniture which actually really helped us. I unpacked the Moses basket and set it up in my bedroom, imagining that one day soon my healthy little baby would be laying in it. I would look at it every day. Our circumstances were now much better to bring a child into, we were both working, we had a suitable home and we had all the items we thought we would need for our baby. We were definitely better prepared for what was to come this time around.

The day of the twenty-week scan came and we made our way to hospital to the maternity department. Again met with the faces of happy couples waiting for their names to be called. On my notes I was down as a high-risk pregnancy and just looking at those words made me feel all the more anxious. It felt like the longest wait we had ever had for a scan but finally my name was called. I went, lay down, and waited for the cold gel to touch my belly and the scan to start. She mentioned how lively our little baby was, she struggled but managed to check all the measurements. All was looking very well. “Would you like a photo?” Of course we would, who wouldn’t? “We’ll get you back in at thirty weeks, we have no concerns but because your high risk we just want to keep a close eye on you”.

I really needed to stop worrying but I couldn’t help it, everything was still so raw and fresh in my mind. My anxiety levels were constantly high. I didn’t really feel much of the excitement that I had before. My bump was really beginning to show and I couldn’t stop touching it. I loved this baby so much. I had barely felt flutters with Imogen, when I started feeling kicks this time it was the most amazing feeling. When I was approaching twenty-six-weeks I started to struggle, I just wanted to pass the gestation of twenty-six plus six which is where I was when Imogen decided to arrive. Although in my time on the neonatal unit I had witnessed a twenty-two-week baby survive all the way through to being ready to be discharged. It is truly amazing what the doctors can do. The milestone came and went and I was soon at thirty-weeks, another scan, another all okay. By now the baby was growing so well, it wasn’t just kicks I was feeling, I could feel the baby pressing its foot into my rib cage, it would push out and bulge through my belly, it was a truly magical feeling. I made it to full term of thirty-seven-weeks and my anxiety suddenly reduced. “You can come any day you want now baby, you’re going to be okay”.

I left going on maternity leave until the very last minute. My home was ready, I had a hospital bag ready. I was three days over my due date. Then suddenly, after the longest nine months I started to feel those pains again. On 11th August 2009, one year to the day I lost my beautiful Imogen, I woke with my waters gone. "Please don't come today baby, it is really not a good day for me". The first anniversary of Imogen's death was so hard, it felt like it had all happened just yesterday, all the feelings felt far too real. But the labour I was clearly now in proved to be a good distraction.

I ended up at the maternity ward that evening, I was having intense and very close contractions. I had to go to the same hospital which I had given birth to Imogen in as I was still considered very high risk. This was a completely new experience, it was all very different to the one I'd had before. I wasn't in a room full of people, it was just Jack and one midwife. I kept looking at the clock praying our baby would stay put till after midnight, but the contractions were really picking up some pace. At 11:56pm I was free from pain, and said in my mind I love you Imogen, for it had now been exactly a year, to the date and time, since her death. 11:57 it picked up again, not yet, please not yet! Then very shortly after midnight on the 12th August 2009 I gave birth to a crying and very healthy baby boy, he was instantly placed in my arms. He was the most beautiful little boy I had ever seen, he was so perfect. The love and joy I felt in that moment was overwhelming, there were tears of happiness rolling down my face when I turned to Jack, "he's healthy Jack, he's crying". He had a good strong healthy set of lungs on him which was everything I had hoped for, we had done it, we were a mummy and daddy again. After he had been thoroughly checked over I was told we could leave this bigger hospital but we had to go over to the local hospital in our home town, just to be checked throughout the day. I got out of the bed, had a shower and got dressed again. We put our gorgeous little baby in his car seat and made our way back to our town.

We were well known on the maternity ward where we lived, all the staff knew our history. They were all so incredibly happy for us. They provided us a private room and I had my little boy lying next to me in his tiny plastic cot. Jack went home to get some sleep, it had been a very long twenty-four hours, full of so many mixed emotions.

Our little boy was just absolutely beautiful, I couldn't take my eyes off him, and I thanked him for holding out until after midnight and, more importantly, for being healthy. I couldn't breast feed. I still had the mental block which had developed when I had expressed for Imogen. I fed him a bottle and changed him, he was incredibly tired too. I lay down and just watched him sleep, hardly believing how lucky I was that he was mine. I slowly drifted off to sleep too. I hadn't felt this content in all of my life. Finally, my life had meaning, a real purpose. I honestly believe my son saved my life, if it wasn't for him, I don't know how much more I could've taken. He's truly my little miracle.

We named our baby Toby. He needed one more check over before we could be discharged and whilst this was going on I looked at his tiny little hands. I noticed he only had one line on his palms. "That's a bit odd isn't it? I haven't seen that before", I said this whilst pointing it out to the midwife. "Everything is looking good so I wouldn't worry about that for now". With that we were discharged, our baby was coming home. We were going home as a family. I was still so incredibly tired, all the excitement and emotions, everything had completely worn me out. When we got home I just held and cuddled Toby, I just couldn't put my sweet little baby boy down, but after his next feed I knew I needed to get some sleep. I fed him and changed him again and carried him upstairs. I sat with him on the edge of my bed still completely mesmerised, then I very gently placed him into the Moses basket. There he was, the most beautiful sight I had seen. My dream, now a reality. I kissed his tiny little forehead, then had a well needed sleep. We were both as tired as each other.

Now we had our beautiful boy everything just seemed perfect, Jack's job was going really well and I was on maternity leave so I could fully focus all of my attention on Toby. I loved all the time that it was just me and him, I couldn't get enough of him. He was just so adorable. I couldn't believe how lucky I was to have such a beautiful, perfect child. He was so content and he very rarely cried, he only did if he was hungry or needed changing. He was an absolute dream to have. I got very good night sleeps; it was the complete opposite to what I had been told about looking after a newborn. Toby would normally only wake once a night, he was such a content little baby. I took to it naturally. I promised him I would never let him down and he would have the life I didn't have. I would give him the world, all the love and all the support he would ever need. All those promises I had made to my future children throughout the years, I would keep every single one of them.

Chapter 10: Turning Point

August 2009

As I had mentioned before, my nanna had always said to me that she wanted to live long enough to meet her first great grandchild. She never met Imogen as her health was quickly deteriorating with age, the journey to London and the emotional stress of it all would have been too much for her to cope with. Nanna was becoming really unwell and she was on medication which had made her skin as thin as tissue paper, she had to be very careful on a daily basis. Mum had come over from Geneva to meet Toby and stay with us for a week. We had made plans to take Toby over to meet nanna, as it was her wish, but I didn't want to take Toby on my own just in case something happened to nanna while we were with her. I put Toby into the car and me and mum made the drive over to see her. When nanna met Toby, it really was such a special moment, she sat on her chair and asked if she could hold him. I very gently placed him in her arms, they were both so fragile. She ever so gently ran her fingers from his forehead down to his chin and said, "he is the most perfect little baby I have ever seen, he is absolutely beautiful". I was so pleased she had finally met him. Mum took a photograph of this very special moment. She had finally got to meet her great- grandchild, her wish came true.

My nanna couldn't hold onto Toby for long and once she was satisfied I carefully took him from her. I hadn't seen her face light up like it had in that moment for a very long time. I think afterwards she wanted a moment to herself as she was a little overwhelmed with emotions. She used to love her plants and used them as an excuse to leave the room. She went outside to water them, as she did every single day. As she was watering, she scraped her leg, so slightly, on a square plant pot, this gentle rub was enough to tear her skin so badly that she needed hospital treatment. Mum rushed her to the hospital and I stayed behind with Toby to clean up the blood, even trying to wash it out from her shoes yet as much as tried, I couldn't get the blood off them. It was so upsetting and I was relieved that mum was there.

They returned a few hours later and nanna's leg had been bandaged up. She needed to be so very careful. We were extremely worried about leaving her on her own but she was adamant that she would be fine. She enjoyed her own space. We went home shortly after as I needed to get Toby back home as it was getting late, but I could not stop worrying about nanna. A couple of days later, mum got a phone call to say that nanna had been admitted to hospital, she had again torn her skin but hopefully she wouldn't be in for too long.

The next morning mums had another call, which really upset hers, I asked what was wrong. "Nanna tried to get out of the bed at the hospital because she needed the toilet and as she did, she went dizzy and fell to the floor. She bled out so much that's she's died". I felt sick, my poor nanna, what a horrific way to die. I can't even imagine how scary that must have been for her. It was only a few days ago that she had met Toby. I wasn't ready to lose her, she had been so lovely to me every time I had seen her. Although she was never too involved, when I did see her, it was so special and our time together always meant a lot to me. I was going to miss her and wished I had seen her more over the years. Her funeral wasn't long after, she was now reunited with grandad.

Toby got bigger by the day, he absolutely loved his sleep, cuddles and food. The health visitor made frequent visits to check his weight and to see how we were all getting on, she was a lovely lady. Toby always seemed to be more interested in watching baby programmes on the TV than playing with toys. He didn't really interact with toys in a way that I expected but figured that was just him. I wondered if a sibling would help so he would have someone else to play with. I spoke to Jack about trying again for another child so Toby wouldn't grow up on his own. Jack didn't need any persuading, he agreed, without hesitation and thought it was a good idea. When he was growing up he had a sibling only eleven months older than him so felt that having two children, close in age, was a good idea.

Our last pregnancy had gone so well that we thought that what had happened with Imogen was a strike of extremely bad luck.

I must have fallen pregnant the first time we tried because when Toby was ten months old I started to feel signs that, once again, I could be pregnant. I took a pregnancy test and it was indeed positive! I thought to myself how it would be lovely if this one was a girl. I longed for a daughter after losing Imogen, but of course either way it didn't really matter, what mattered to me most of all was the good health of the baby. With this third pregnancy I wasn't feeling as well as when I was carrying Toby. The morning sickness was terrible and the tiredness was rather extreme. It turned out that I was suffering from an iron deficiency again so I was prescribed tablets for that. I was put down as a normal pregnancy because of my pregnancy with Toby, I was no longer classed as high risk. The first scan at twelve weeks was fine and the due date was the same day as Jack's birthday, what an amazing gift that would be if we had the baby on that date. I felt a lot more relaxed this time around. I was excited that we were expecting again but I also told Jack not to hold his breath about sharing a birthday, everyone knows babies are, very rarely, born on their due date.

I was eager this time around to know what the gender of the baby was, and I had done some research and found a business that offered 4D baby scans and gender reveal. I just had to book the appointment, thinking what a lovely experience it would be. I booked an appointment for the earliest point this type of scan could be done, which was sixteen weeks.

On the date of the 4D scan I was so excited, I was still constantly wondering if we were having a boy or a girl. We made our way over to where the scan company were based. It was not at all the same environment as the hospital scans were. It was a very calm and relaxing place, with soothing music playing quietly in the background. The waiting area was very small and cosy. As it was an appointment service, there was only one other couple in the waiting room. My name was called right on time that the appointment was for. The room we went into was very tranquil, much like what you would expect if you were going for a massage for example. It was very nice indeed, I felt quite posh and privileged as in my mind we had just gone private and away from the normal health service. Obviously this was a one off, but it was nice to feel that way, if only for a short time.

I lay on the bed and the lady talked us through the process, telling us that the service was in no way a medical one, it was purely to enjoy seeing our baby in 4D and to disclose the gender. As she placed the instrument on my belly, she went straight to our baby's face, "he looks like me", I said. The details were so incredibly clear, we could easily see the shape of this tiny little face, a cute little button nose, big eyes and adorable thin little lips. My heart just melted. "Would you like to know the gender of your baby?", she said with a lovely warm smile across her face, "yes please, we're really excited to find out". "You're having a baby boy". Oh my goodness, another boy! It was such lovely news, I felt so lucky that we were having another healthy baby and we already knew he was super cute.

"Well that's handy isn't it Jack? We already have everything we need for a boy". The whole experience was one of the best I'd had throughout any of my pregnancies. Two little boys, I was sure they would grow up to be the best of friends.

We still had the routine twenty-week scan, everything again was perfect but one of the aspects of the appointment had changed. As we were having the scan at the hospital we were asked if we wanted to know the gender! I thought to myself that it was sod's law! Never before had they disclosed this information and now we had paid someone else to find out, they were offering to tell us. "We had a private scan and were told we're having a boy?". "Yes, you're definitely having a boy, that's very clear!".

I didn't need any more scans throughout the remainder of the pregnancy as everything was going so well. All I had to do from then on was attend the routine antenatal appointments. As this time, I was considered a low-risk pregnancy, I was just put under the care of the maternity team at our local hospital, I was also able to plan to give birth to our baby boy there. I was so pleased that this was now the scenario we were facing. With each pregnancy the whole process seemed to get so much easier.

Becoming a mother was the best thing that ever happened to me, I doted on Toby, he was an absolute treasure. We would joke that we had been really lucky with him and what if our expectant baby was the stereotypical sleepless nights child?

Toby was now over a year old. I always believed baby's start to walk around this age, but he wasn't yet walking, just crawling everywhere at great speed. He would toddle around whilst holding onto the sofa, but he would not walk independently. I tried encouraging him to use his first steps baby walker, but he wouldn't. Maybe he was just going to be late walker, so I wasn't going to worry too much. All babies learn to do things in their own time. Because Toby wasn't yet walking, we bought a double buggy. I knew I was going to have my hands full, but I didn't want it any other way. I felt so incredibly lucky.

Jack's birthday came around but guess what didn't? Our baby was just too comfortable inside my belly, he clearly wasn't coming on his due date though I did go into labour two days later. I asked my brother Tom if he could stay at mine to look after Toby whilst I went into hospital, he dropped everything and arrived as soon as he could. I had already phoned the maternity ward to give them the heads up that I was in the early stages of labour, they knew I was familiar with the childbirth process and asked me to stay at home for as long as I could. We sat with Tom talking and drinking cups of teas until around midnight when I thought I'd better go. My contractions were then only a couple of minutes apart so we were getting very close to meeting our son. Toby was sound asleep in his cot and Tom said he would sleep on the sofa, telling us not to worry about a thing.

Jack grabbed my hospital bag and the paperwork we needed and we gave the maternity ward another call to let them know that we were on our way. It was so nice to be having our baby so locally, it was only a five-minute drive in the car. We arrived and made our way to the ward, we were so familiar with it as we had already spent so much time there. We were booked in and led to one of the side rooms where I was quickly examined. I was already 9cms dilated, we really had got there at the very last minute. Within an hour I had given birth to another beautiful son. His features were entirely different to Toby, he really took after me. I was so incredibly happy, what a beautiful gift in life my babies were. I dressed him in the cutest little blue sleep suit, he was so tired bless him. I just couldn't put him down. It made me realise that they don't stay that little for very long at all, Toby was so big in comparison.

We were told that because I already had a child at home we wouldn't need to stay in long, we could be discharged once I'd had a shower. I passed our beautiful boy over to Jack whilst I got myself sorted out. Within four hours of arriving at the hospital we were able to take our newest addition to the family home. I had never gone through this process as quickly, it was such a lovely experience. With every pregnancy the experience had become better and better. We put our tiny, beautiful baby in his car seat and left the hospital.

At home Tom was asleep on the sofa and Toby hadn't woken up once. I gently woke Tom up, he looked at us and then looked at the time, "wow that was quick". I felt as though I had bragging rights to being the quickest mother in history to have a child in hospital and to already be at home again. "Here he is, say hello to baby John". Tom was so pleased to meet him and couldn't wait for a cuddle with his new little nephew. "Thank you so much for looking after Toby for us, you really helped us out there". Tom said it was his pleasure and he was just happy to be there with us. He stayed for another cup of tea and then made his way home. The sun was starting to come up and we were all extremely tired.

John had a feed and we headed for bed, checking on Toby just to make sure he was okay. He didn't know that he was a big brother yet. I smiled from cheek to cheek with a feeling of contentment that our little family was complete. The Moses basket was back out and already for John to sleep in beside our bed. Exactly as I had done with Toby, I carefully placed John into it, feeling like the luckiest person in the world. I now had two healthy and very beautiful boys.

Foolishly I had thought to myself before I had John, 'what's two children when you already have one, seriously, how hard can it be?' The answer to that is it is hard! I had a newborn and an eighteen-month-old. John was indeed the stereotypical baby, my gosh he really let you know if he needed something. John loved his food and cuddles just like his brother Toby, but their personalities were already showing themselves to be two entirely different characters. I realised very early on that my assumption of having two babies close in age does not necessarily mean they will be close and best friends.

My concern over Toby not walking did increase. The health visitor wasn't concerned about anything regarding John but Toby wasn't reaching certain milestones, I wasn't overly worried, I just thought that he would do things in his own time. Of course he did eventually take his first steps but he still wasn't interacting with toys in the ways that were expected. This was concerning as it was affecting the development of his fine motor skills. I didn't really take much notice of what the health visitor was telling me because, to me, Toby was as perfect as perfect could be. John seemed to be developing at a particularly faster rate than Toby had, but I concluded that this was because he had his older brother to copy and learn from whereas Toby had to learn it all himself, hence the delayed development.

My older brother, Tom had met a South African girl. They were getting married in South Africa and were going to pay for the family to travel over for the wedding and spend a two-week holiday together. The thought of it with two very young children did slightly concern me, but this was my brother's wedding and I wasn't going to miss it, it was also the holiday of my dreams, we'd be going on a real safari.

I needed to get passports organised but never realised how hard it would be to get the photos of both the boys, they wouldn't stay still for a second. I managed it though and the passports were issued.

The day of our holiday of a lifetime quickly came. I had packed two-weeks prior so we were extremely well organised and more than ready to go. The boys were really very good especially when you take into consideration how long the flight was. It took a total of twenty-three hours from leaving our home to reaching our destination. It was absolutely exhausting but totally worth it, I was feeling so incredibly lucky that we were having this experience.

The first day we went to stay at a lodge in a safari resort. The hot water system was a tin barrel heated by fire. The fire would be lit very early in the morning by the people who worked there. It had solid wooden beds for the children and a big king size wooden bed for us. The bathroom was modern, it wasn't how I had imagined it would be. I sat outside that evening, the sky was a blanket of stars, it was such a beautiful sight. I could hear a lot of noises from animals in the distance, I couldn't tell you what animals they were, though I did recognise the constant sound of grasshoppers, it was such a surreal experience. I couldn't quite believe where we were, it just didn't seem real, it felt as though we were living a dream.

The next morning we woke up early because we were going on a safari, a real African safari! It was so incredibly exciting. Between us all we had two 4x4's, each one driven by a tour ranger. Toby and John were surprisingly taking everything in, even with them being so young they seemed to realise that what we were experiencing was incredibly special. We didn't see any lions, but we did see a lot of wildebeest, they were everywhere. The whole safari experience truly was a dream come true.

Jack found it difficult to be around my family constantly for two whole weeks. He made it very clear to me that although the entire holiday had been paid for by my brother, he was doing me a favour just by being there. As soon as we were alone Jack would make snide little digs. I was not going to let him spoil the experience we were having though, it was unlikely we have an experience like this one again.

We did so much whilst we were in South Africa, the wedding was simply beautiful and it was set in such a stunning location. My now sister-in-law looked absolutely stunning in her dress, she was just beaming with happiness, as was my brother. I was so incredibly happy that we were able to share their special day with them.

One part of the holiday was a mental turning point in my life. The Oribi Gorge has the largest gorge swing in the world, it is a 165-meter swing and is the equivalent of jumping off a fifty-five storey high building. We were booked to do it, we must have be crazy! As I was getting harnessed up I thought to myself, if I live I'll be mum to the boys, but if I die, I'll be mum to Imogen. Completely crazy thoughts I know, but that was what ran through my mind at that time. I had never done anything like the Oribi Gorge before and I doubted I would ever get the chance again, so I went for it.

There was a short ladder down the side of the gorge to where the swing was and a small waterfall, it was refreshing feeling the splashes of water from it in the soaring South African heat. I felt a rope be attached to the back of the harness I was wearing, the rope went tight and the guide asked me if I was ready, I nodded. "3,2,1 JUMP!" and with a push off the side of the gorge, I was free falling. It was the most amazing feeling I have ever felt! I started to swing backwards and forwards so close to brushing the treetops just below me, then very quickly after, I was very slowly pulled back up to the top of the gorge. The jump took seconds but strangely the getting back up part was much scarier, the adrenaline wore off and the reality hit. It took a full five minutes to be pulled back to the start point. "How was it?", asked Jack. "That was AMAZING! Your turn, are you ready?". Jack did the jump too, I felt so grateful I'd had the opportunity, I won't ever forget it.

Our last stop on the holiday was to a lion reserve. As we approached the resort there were ostriches roaming, it was quite a sight. The resort itself was an amazing experience, they bred lions to get the population numbers up, they were not free but did have a whole lot of land to roam on. We arrived and checked ourselves in to our accommodation. Tom told me that you could stroke and sit with baby lions, I just had to do it. The lion cubs were almost six months old so being able to handle them wouldn't have been possible if they were much older. We went into the enclosure and there we were, sitting around little baby lions. They were just adorable, I took a lot of photos of Toby and John with the cubs, they were really enjoying stroking them, Toby was absolutely fascinated by it all. I sat beside one of the cubs and I began to stroke it as though I was just stroking a domestic pet, the cub started licking my hand, I was being licked by a lion! I can't say how incredible that experience was. Whilst we were there we were able to visit the cubs at any time we wanted. This particular resort was very noisy with the sound of animals, they really came to life at night, I honestly thought a herd of zebra were stampeding behind our lodge, I wouldn't dare to go outside that night.

As amazing as South Africa was to visit, there were some moments where I didn't feel entirely safe, so I'm not sure we would ever go again, we had two minibuses as there were so many in our group and when we reached traffic lights in Johannesburg, people would bang on the vehicle begging for money. We were also followed by someone asking for money when went into a supermarket. We were asked if we wanted to buy a taser whilst walking through a shopping centre car park in a place called Newcastle. Also, in Newcastle Jack decided he didn't want to stay at my now sister-in-law's, families house. We found accommodation nearby with a pool which was fairly cheap, but we ended up having a security guard at our room all night as people were trying to get to us, that was pretty scary. We also stayed at a house which belonged to a friend of my sister-in-law in a place called Margate. Someone broke in whilst we were there. This was all within our two-week trip.

With all that aside, we were all okay and the good things of the holiday outweighed the bad experiences. When our holiday came to an end, we were able to take home the most amazing memories which would last a lifetime. The holiday shifted a lot of my thoughts. Until that point, I had always been very up and down with depression, this was certainly a turning point in a mental sense for me. Sadly, mine and Jack's relationship was now hitting an all-time low. Which was a shame because since having Toby and John we had been getting on a whole lot better.

Chapter 11: Breaking Point

March 2013

There was only so much time I could take off work with maternity leave. I had to work out how to care for our two young children as obviously Jack still had to go to work. I went back on very reduced hours and whilst I was at work, Jacks sister would kindly babysit our two boys. Jack's sister helped us with the children so much and never asked for anything in return, she absolutely loved having them both and the boys enjoyed being with their auntie.

Mine and Jack's relationship was now almost nonexistent, we weren't really getting on at all. I really didn't want my children to grow up in any environment similar to the one I had. A toxic household is no good for anyone. My children meant too much to me to put them through a life where they wouldn't grow up happy, it really wouldn't be healthy for them and I knew that. I wasn't in the right state of mind when I had the boys, not in a way that was damaging to them, but I was still grieving when I fell pregnant. We had an extremely complicated relationship. It had started as a dream, I believed that we could build a life together because we had both started life with difficult circumstances, that mindset in me had now drastically changed since becoming a mother. It wasn't just me anymore, in my mind I didn't matter that much. I had my children to think about now and they deserved so much better. They didn't deserve the life I had accepted and created for myself.

Jack really didn't do anything to help, I felt as though I did it all and I did. I would do everything for the children as well as all the washing, cleaning, shopping, cooking - I could go on but you get the idea. Jack would come home from work in his dirty, oil ridden overalls and he would walk mud and oil into the house. He would go straight into the kitchen and empty his pockets on the kitchen worktop. He literally left a mess everywhere he went in the home. He would barely interact with the boys, it was almost as though they didn't even exist. It just wasn't right. If I ever said anything it would always start an argument. I remembered how I had felt all those times he had let me down before. I remember how he had pretty much forced me into a relationship with him by threatening his own life against me. I couldn't deal with him and do my absolute best for the boys. Jack was also still not helping me at all with the repayments for Imogen's funeral, it had now been three years and I still had a lot left to pay. I still couldn't afford to buy her a headstone.

I'd had enough, it was clear to me he wouldn't ever change and it was probably wrong of me to expect him too. Our relationship was past fixing, I stopped loving

him when he left Imogen and I in hospital. I just couldn't love him again. The next time he started an argument I asked him to leave, but he wouldn't. The boys were in bed and we had a huge row. He pinned me up against the kitchen wall, I was so scared when it got like this. To feel trapped in your own home is such a difficult way to live. I just wanted him to go and leave us all alone. He must have known that I didn't love him anymore, why was he still there? He wasn't interested in me and I wasn't interested in him anymore. He was messaging so many other women on his phone surly one of them want him?

I would say things to really push his buttons, really nasty things to try to get him to leave. I told him that there were more people dead than alive that cared about him, that did it. I felt terrible saying those words but I was desperate. Those words cut him deep and he did walk out. I quickly locked the doors behind him. Had I finally got what I wanted?

Him leaving brought a huge sense of relief, but what I didn't know was that he was close by waiting for an opportunity to get back into the house. I unlocked the kitchen door and went to go outside. That's when he came from nowhere and pushed me, with force, back into the house. I fell backwards onto the kitchen floor and hit my head against the wall. "I'm not going anywhere; those are my kids upstairs and I have as

much right to be here as you do!". I was always going to feel, and be, trapped by him. He was always up to no good behind my back, the messages to other women had been going on since the day we got together. He made me look like such a fool and I felt like one too.

Jack had to go to work in America for a month, there were thousands of flood damaged cars and he was called on to help with the processing of them all. I was so thankful that we were going to have a break away from him, I really couldn't wait for him to go. It was January and Toby was already three I had to get him into a nursery. Whilst Jack was away I coped really well, better than I thought I would with two very young children, things were so much easier to keep on top of, the house was easier to clean, there was less washing to do. Above all those things there was a sense of calm, peace and serenity. It was so amazing to feel like that, for the first time in my life I felt a contentment that I had never felt before. I was content with my children. I realised even more then how little Jack did, he did nothing when he was with us. I knew now for sure that I could cope and manage on my own. Marley was still a big part of my life and we would often meet up, she was never too far away. I knew that with her support we would be fine.

Toby's first day of nursery came and I was so nervous, would he be looked after and cared for how I cared for

him? Would he be happy, would he enjoy it? I cried when he went in. Last time a child of mine was in the care of other people they never came home. The experience I had with Imogen branched off into so many other aspects of my life. Waiting for Toby to finish nursery for the day felt like the longest three hours of my life. I assumed it would all go well. When I went to pick him up, I was taken into an office, "we have some concerns regarding Toby, he doesn't seem to be at similar stages to his peers". How could they say that about my perfect boy, what on earth did they think could be wrong with him? Children were all different and all developed at different rates didn't they? I started to dread dropping Toby off to nursery because almost every day after picking him up the staff had words with me. Long story short. He was referred to paediatrics and an A.D.O.S assessment was arranged.

Jack came back from America and I told him what had been happening with Toby but he wasn't taking any of it in. He wasn't interested in supporting me through any of it and I dealt with all the nursery and hospital appointments on my own. He just shrugged everything off in a 'not my problem' sort of way. I can't tell you how upsetting it is when you're learning there is something very different with your child. Why my child? Why did it have to be my child again?

The day of Toby's assessment came so I drove him to the medical centre. He seemed to do well. I really did not think he had any condition at all. Now all I had to do was wait to hear and carry on as we were until then.

Within a couple of weeks, a letter came from the medical centre, it was the results from Toby's assessment. I opened it right away expecting to read what I had previously assumed. However, what I was expecting wasn't the case. He had been diagnosed as a person with autism. On first instincts, obviously I was upset, it was a shock. Jack still wasn't taking anything seriously; he just wasn't getting involved in any way and he was no support whatsoever. Again, why my child? Why me again? Once I had time to reflect, I soon came to realise that Toby was perfect as he was, well, at home with me he was. The problem was with him not being able to conform with the outside world. I began to realise as John was getting bigger that the differences between the two boys were actually quite significant. I did however think that Toby wasn't as bad as I was being told and I wanted him to have as normal a life as possible. I wanted him to go to mainstream school with his brother.

That proved to be one of the biggest mistakes I ever made. I should have listened to what people were telling me but I had trust issues with believing what I was told, as I said this stemmed back to when Imogen was in my life. The professionals were completely wrong about her so they could also be wrong about Toby too. He was my son and I knew him better than anyone. I ignored the advice of putting Toby straight into a special educational needs school and instead placed him in the local mainstream school which was situated very close to our home. He had a one-to-one assistant and an education and health care plan that the school would follow, everything was in place for him. Toby would be happy in mainstream school with certain provisions in place for him.

The first couple of years I had little to no concerns. I was still being spoken too regularly by staff members at Toby's school, it was never anything positive either. It all became extremely draining. At home Toby was fine and appeared to be happy at school so I stuck with my original decision and kept the mainstream placement.

John started nursery within the same school and I thought we were absolutely on the right track, it was seemingly working well. I believed both the boys were really happy and enjoying their early school life. We only lived a two-minute walk away so the school run wasn't any stress.

Meanwhile Jack and I, still living together in a weird, complex, should have ended years ago relationship were 'surprisingly' (sorry for the sarcasm) not getting along at all. We had been sleeping in separate rooms for quite some time. I was co sleeping with John. Jack was staying in John's bedroom. Toby slept well on his own in his room, he really liked his own space. We put up blackout blinds because if the sun was up, so was Toby. He didn't seem to need much sleep at all. If it wasn't for the blackout blinds during the summer when the days were long, Toby would never sleep.

I was in Toby's room tidying up his toys and Jack was downstairs, it was May 2013. My phone rang and the caller I.D was Max. It was unusual, normally I communicated with Max through messages, he very rarely called. I answered the call very quietly as I didn't want Jack to hear that I was on the phone, I just knew that if he did it would start, yet another argument. "Hi Max, what's up?".

"Marley, I want you to hear this from me before you hear it from anyone else". He had recently told me he was having pains and after a lot of doctor visits they thought it may be gallstones. "I have bowel cancer and it's spread, pretty badly". I couldn't believe what I was hearing, I didn't know what to say, it hit me like a lightning bolt, straight through my heart. "I am so sorry Max, thank you for telling me, if there is anything I can do please just say, I'm here for you".

I was numb, I had always thought an awful lot of Max, he had been one of the best friends I'd had and I had done nothing for him in return for the kindness he had shown me throughout the years. He genuinely was one of the nicest people I had ever met, the person who would do anything for anyone, who would always listen and support anyone. I had to find a way of being there for him when he needed his friends the most. But Jack didn't know the history between us. He knew we were friends, but he didn't know we had worked together, he didn't know he wanted to be with me and I had turned him down because he deserved more in his life than damaged goods. I was so scared for him, I knew from what he had said that the prognosis wasn't good, but there was always hope.

My brain would not switch off. I began to question why I had ever been so stupid when I could have had a great life with Max. We could have had children together. I would have noticed that he wasn't well a lot sooner and helped him to get the support he needed. My children were happy but they didn't have the life I'd hoped to give them. What a mess I had created. I knew it was all created through the choices I had made in life. I had so far made so many bad choices. I always knew deep down that when I was making certain life choices that they weren't the right ones, it was all down to having very little self-worth. Max had said to me before that he'd had relationships, but no one compared to me. I was in turmoil once more. Max was now fighting for his life, he didn't deserve this, he deserved the best in life. I always wanted the absolute best for him.

Max phoned me on the Friday and on the Sunday, I was at work, my manager also knew Max really well and was also very worried about him. There were four of us in work that day and because it wasn't busy, my manager and I called Max and asked if we could pop over together to see him, thankfully he said it was fine. We went straight to his house to show our support and let him know we were there for him. It was so upsetting talking to him about it, we tried to keep the conversation as light as possible and keep off the subject. Max didn't really want to discuss it and suggested we treat him as normal and have a normal conversation, understandably but also frustratingly, he just wanted to keep his mind off it.

I went to see him a few times in the following months but he was deteriorating so very fast. It was unbelievably heartbreaking to see. Before long he was in a hospice, his days were now very limited. He was only thirty-two years old, that's no age at all, he was still so very young. I asked Jack to drive me to the hospice so I could say goodbye to my friend. It was 30th October 2013. I went in and Max was looking so very frail, not what you would expect someone his age to look like. The illness had ravaged his entire body. I think he was upset with me as that's how it felt, he didn't want to say goodbye, he still wanted to have a normal conversation with his friend and be treated normally. I tried so hard but there was so much I wanted to say but I just couldn't. When my time was up I held his hand, kissed his cheek and said goodbye to my good friend for the very last time in person. I didn't know then that it was the last time. I sent him messages after asking if I could come and see him again but there were either other people there or he just wasn't well enough. He very sadly passed away on 9th December 2013. I was beyond heartbroken, I was absolutely devastated. He meant so much more to me than I had ever allowed myself to believe.

Max's funeral was so hard, my manager from work accompanied me. I just couldn't hold it together no matter how hard I tried. I don't know if anyone ever knew the truth between me and Max. I often think of him, even now I miss him terribly.

Jack was being increasingly difficult and I had no patience for him left in me. We had yet another almighty row and I told him I should have never been with him all these years, I should have been with Max. Max was gone and Jack was still here making my life hell. I told him everything. He had no idea about any of what had been going on in my mind. I had now been in a relationship with Jack for thirteen years, and each and every one of those years had been hard, he had drained me so much. He had made my life difficult beyond belief. We were not growing into an amazing, happy life together. I put all my energy, everything I had into doing what was right for everyone else. I had never, ever done what was right for me and to be brutally honest I had quite frankly had it!

I'd had enough of all the drama in my life, how much is one person meant to endure? All my life it had been one thing after another. All I tried to do was my absolute best by people but no one did their best for me, no one! I tried to think positively. I tried to think that if I kept going and worked hard things would one day work out. I was once the little girl who vowed to give her children a better life, a life full of love, joy and abundance in all areas. I did not want them to have a life like mine and end up growing up broken. This life I was living was not that life I had always dreamt of. All I wanted was a happy life for me and my children. Did I really not deserve that, did my children not deserve that? My reality was very difficult. I knew at many points if I'd had a different mindset my life could have been very different. I'd had opportunities, I'd passed up opportunities for a feeling of lack of worth. It wasn't just me now, I had two beautiful children and one with special needs that I had to take into consideration. I decided I was going to put me first, I needed to make drastic changes.

I also had a thought that because I had denied any relationship with Max, I had taken away his chance of a family and true love. I had always been good enough; I just couldn't see things for what they truly were. My choices hadn't only impacted my life but also the lives of others too.

Jack came home from work one day and told me he had lost his job, that was what tipped me over the edge. I couldn't take any more. My mind instantly went back to the day that we were driving home from the hospital after losing Imogen and finding out I was going back to nothing, not even a home. I couldn't deal with that again. All those feelings of absolute despair came flooding back. It sent my mind racing, so much I even went light headed . It's surprising how after traumatic times a single word can trigger such intense reactions.

After another argument I asked Jack once again to leave us, we had two beautiful children and we had to think about them now. I had never known anyone so irresponsible. That was the end of our relationship and there was absolutely nothing left. I didn't want Toby and John to grow up in a toxic relationship. Jack did not take it well at all, he was more worried about himself. He knew he had forced me into being with him before, I wasn't going to let him do it do me again. He would often sit outside the house parked in his car. One day when he had been out drinking, he came to the house and started banging on the window, I opened the door and he stumbled in. He was again threatening to take his own life. Like countless times before he started grabbing hold of me and holding me up against the wall whilst shouting in my face. He briefly let go of me and I ran upstairs to lock myself in the toilet so I could call the police, I couldn't deal with this on my own. I just wanted him to leave me alone. I got as far as typing 99 into my phone when the door was kicked in, he grabbed me and grabbed my phone off me and put it in his pocket. I watched the phone fly out of its case but he was so intoxicated he didn't realise. He thought he had my phone but he didn't, all he had was the case. I made a mental note of where the phone was in the hope I could get away from him soon and long enough to make the call to the police. For four hours he was talking me down, shouting at me, chasing me around the house, pushing me against furniture with such force it would break. He grabbed the landline phone ripping the cables from the wall ensuring I had no way to call for help. We ended up in the kitchen and my glass fruit bowl went flying, he grabbed a large shard of glass and went to slice his neck with it, I put my hand out to stop him and it caught me, I now had a 5cm gash in my hand and it was pouring with blood. Jack said, "I'm sorry, I'm sorry but you won't listen, you and those boys mean the world to me I promise things will get better". I was listening but I couldn't believe him, so many times I'd heard those words before, that's all they were, words, nothing ever actually changed. I told him I needed to go to the toilet, this time he let me go. I grabbed my phone from where it fell at the top of the stairs and went to the toilet. I finally managed to call the police. I couldn't talk to them, the walls were paper thin, all I had to say was yes to confirm I needed help and yes again to the confirm the address.

Luckily enough the boys were asleep throughout the duration of what happened. I said to Jack that I was sorry, but I just couldn't cope anymore, we weren't good together and we all deserved better, even Jack. I couldn't help the fact that I didn't love him anymore, all that love had been destroyed. It was now 4am and he was telling me he was going to go and end his life. I told him not to go, that he needed to think about things, that everything would work out for the best, to stay for a bit and calm down. We were sitting at the bottom of the stairs and the front door was wide open. He noticed I kept looking out the front door and asked who I was waiting for, with that a police car pulled up and Jack bolted out the back door. Two officers came in and I told them he'd legged it, that the only way out was through the ally. They checked but he was nowhere to be seen. He had jumped the back garden fence and gone through the neighbours garden. He was long gone. They could see something had happened, my landline phone cables ripped out was one of the first things the officers eyes were drawn to, the broken furniture I had fallen against, the broken glass in the kitchen, the large gash on my hand, I was asked if I needed hospital treatment but I couldn't, I was on my own with the boys, what would happen to them? so I refused. They asked to check the welfare of the children and went upstairs to their rooms and found them soundly asleep. Noticing the toilet door kicked in and broken.

The officers were very concerned for my wellbeing and knew from experience that Jack would come back. One officer stayed with me whilst the other went to hide the police car around the corner. The officer who stayed with me said, "this is very important, do exactly what I tell you to do. He will phone you, you have to say to him that the police have gone as they were called to another job. Tell him it's safe to come back". Within minutes of that conversation my phone rang, it was Jack. "I can't believe you did that!". I said, "I'm sorry, I didn't know what else to do, they have gone now, they had another job". He didn't believe me at first, then he said okay and started making his way back to the house. One officer hid under the glass of the back door in the kitchen, the other waited on the stairwell by the front door. I heard a scuffle from the kitchen, "I've got him!". The officer with me ran through to the kitchen. Jack just looked at me with a look I had never seen before, it was a scary look as though he was telling me I was going to pay for this. Jack was arrested there and then. I was overcome with so many feelings. How had it come to this? I had never wanted the police involved. But it really was, at that time, my only option.

The following day welfare officers came to see me and asked if I wanted to press charges against Jack, I said no, I didn't want that at all. I did ask if they could ask him to leave me alone and just give me some space. We were over and this was not the first time I had asked him to leave. Jack did take notice of the officers and began accepting the separation. He temporarily moved in with his sister and very soon after met someone else who he later married.

I also started to move on. I found being a single mum to my boys a lot less stressful than when Jack was living with us. I was still on reduced hours at work but receiving state benefits. I had paid a lot in to the system over the years and now I needed the help, I was grateful for all I got. I was able to see my friends a lot more than I had in a very long time. Every time I had been out before, it didn't matter who I was with or where I was going, Jack always had a problem with it and made my life difficult. Even on the occasions I would visit my brother Tom, Jack would kick off and make things difficult for me. I had got to the stage where I didn't have much care for his outbursts. There comes a point, when you lose feelings for someone, and they don't affect you in the same way.

There was a time, where everything he would say got to me. I would do everything I could to keep him happy, unfortunately that also meant my relationships with friends and family were impacted. It was all because he liked the control he had. As soon as he lost that control, he got worse. But then it reached the point I just couldn't be in the same house as him.

Reflection

I often reflect on my life and I've often heard the phrase, 'everything happens for a reason'. Now, I find it hard to accept that saying, but at the same time, I wonder if I have found some form of truth in those words. Let me explain my thoughts around that.
When I was younger, I endured a childhood with alcohol and abuse. I was accustomed to this treatment by people who said they loved me. Much like my relationship with Jack. It was familiar treatment towards me. Was my childhood preparation for my future relationship? They say girls end up with people who treat them like their father did. That was very close to the truth in this instance. Was the abuse I received as a child the reason for accepting the abuse in my early adult life? I believe that is the case.

The next thing I ponder on is the isolation I experienced as a child and also the time of isolation in the bedsit and flat. Were those experiences preparing me for the six month isolation I had with Imogen in London? That was indeed a very difficult situation but I was fairly well equipped, mentally, to handle it.

That leads me to the strength I had to find within myself to stay with Imogen. It was incredibly hard, but also very natural. Were the combined experience's providing me with the strength that I needed?

Then, the biggest wonder of them all. What reason was it for me to lose my child? Was it to remind me to always be a good parent? Was it to show me that there is no one else more important than your own child, that any child is a precious gift? Was the experience the reason my mindset changed to want a better life for myself and my children? If I hadn't lost Imogen, what would my mindset be? Would I have continued to put up with Jack before my own and our children's happiness? That was the time Jack let me down the most and he also let Imogen down. His excuse was he always expected her to come home, and that is why he wasn't there.

I have had reoccurring thoughts, since a child, that I should share my experiences in some way, in the hope that I might, in my own way help someone else. There have been multiple opportunities where things could have been so very different, what I hope is, that it is recognised where those opportunities were. Because if they are, then maybe it will help someone else to just stop and change the direction that their life is heading towards and save them from further suffering. It seems like unless the mindset of your own self-worth is changed, one bad experience will inevitably lead on to more bad experiences. However, once the mindset is changed and you learn to value yourself more, it will produce the opposite effect, meaning, one good thing happens and that in turn will lead to more good things happening.

I really hope that people understand that they are good enough, but if at this current moment they aren't feeling that way, please stay true to yourself as much as possible and don't get drawn in to being anything other than yourself. Make the choices you truly feel are right for you. Life is always going to have ups and downs. Personally, I would now much prefer a life with more ups.

I thank you for staying with me this far, it's been a difficult journey. Stay with me just a bit longer, things are about to get so much better. It will also really back up the truth in all I've just said mentioned above.

Chapter 12: Hello My Love

August 2014

The boys were staying with Jack for the weekend and I had a night out arranged with my best friend Marley, my first night out in a very long time. Marley has always been there for me when I needed her, the number of times I went to her crying over Jack, she's one of the very few people who know the truth.

I was one of the last of our friends to arrive, we were all meeting at Marley's sisters house. They had already started pre night out drinks and I had some catching up to do. Marley's dad was giving us a lift down to town where the pubs were, right where my old bedsit was.

It felt so different now, we were all thirty years old, last time I'd been out downtown I was only seventeen. I remember years ago joking that over twenty-five nights were grab a granny night, now we were the granny's! We went to a couple of pubs, it was so nice to get out and have a nice time. I definitely was in need for it. I'd missed having time with my friends so much. Everything was going to be different from now on, not being out with the girls all the time but putting myself and my children first. We were going to have a happier and a more balanced life.

Whilst we were out a message came through to my phone asking what I was up to? It was from someone I'd recently added as a friend on social media. All those years ago when I worked in retail, I used to hang out at a garage after work where one of my friends worked, you could say it was a social hub. There were quite a few of us who used to meet up there. One day, rather unexpectedly the garage was taken over by new owners. I wasn't aware of this until the new owner's son walked in, he walked past us all in the reception area, went over to the desk, took a look at all of us sitting there chatting and said, "you lot, get the hell out of my garage!". With that we all quickly legged it, ran to our cars and got away from the place. It was quite a comical moment looking back. I later found out that this same young man, who kicked us all out his garage, was called Mick. When I was working in communications Mick was one of my clients who recognised me from that day.

Fast forward twelve years, the message I had just received was from Mick. Yes, the one who kicked me and my friends out his garage. I replied, confused as to why he had just messaged me, "just out with my friends, what about you?". From then on myself and Mick messaged each other frequently. I used to look forward to his messages, they really made me smile. We would text each other for hours of an evening, I really enjoyed talking to him.

Then one day we arranged to meet up. It was exciting but scary too. I'd spoken to him so many times in person, but that was in a professional manor, this was personal and felt really different. I had only been in an on and off relationship with only Jack since I was seventeen, so thirteen years with the same person. Meeting someone new was way out of my comfort zone.

I had recently read a book called 'Love Life, Live Life' written by Sue Stone. Sue's book teaches you about the techniques she used to turn her own life around from a state of desperation to a life full of abundance. Whilst reading her book I had so many lightbulb moments, everything I read made so much sense and I began using Sue's life transforming techniques within my own life. I learnt so much from reading it and really believe what I learnt completely changed my life. I began telling myself over and over again that I was good enough, I was not damaged goods, I was a happy, caring, loving and a loyal person, If Mick was right for me, I'd give it a go, I WAS good enough.

Mick came across as a really lovely man, my mind was still reluctant to let me believe otherwise and was constantly telling me that he is too good for me, again I would have to remind myself of the mistakes from my past, no Marley, just stop it... I WAS good enough. It was a very tough battle I had with myself. I was used to a completely different way of living. I knew the negative thoughts and feelings were because of the way I had been made to feel about myself. I was consciously choosing something different in the hope that it would eventually alter my current circumstances and ultimately completely change my way of life.

I did everything I could to try and remain in good spirits, making myself feel as good as I could feel. I was grateful for all I had, my now peaceful life, my beautiful children, a social life, a job, my home, my car, I had a lot to be thankful for.

I took a huge leap of faith and invited Mick round. We had been talking for so long over text it just seemed the right thing to do. We would talk for hours, I'd never met anyone as lovely as him and couldn't believe my luck, he made me laugh so much, no one had ever been like this with me before. I was falling for him.

One of the most interesting things I learnt through our chats was that he had spent a part of his life caring for a youngster with autism, he just seemed perfect for me and for my children. I was really hoping this relationship would work out, we just clicked. He had never had children of his own but he knew I had Toby and John and I openly told him that Toby was autistic. It didn't faze him at all, instead he was looking forward to meeting them.

Mick was so kind, caring and compassionate. He was a little on the chubby side but he told me he was a teddy bear and that was just his stuffing. He was able to turn anything into a joke.

I had been told by Jack repeatedly that I was a mess and that no one would want me, who would want to be with a state like me. Mick told me I was beautiful, but he did also say I was far too skinny and he would make me put on some weight. He wasn't wrong about that, I had been underweight for years and I wasn't happy with how it made me look. I felt like everyone who saw me judged me on my weight. Remember Jack used to call me Annie, short for Annie-rexic.

When I was a little girl there was absolutely no possibility of changing my circumstances, I didn't have the power over my own life then. I made a conscious decision when I was around seven years old that, one day, when the time was right I would write a book and share it with the world. I would write a book in the hope that if I could just help one person and give them any hope and help, then it would be worth it. Although I didn't know it then, or understand for that matter, I always lived my life in complete awareness. I was always fully aware of what was happening and no pain could ever permanently hurt the person I was deep down, no one could hurt the spirit of who I was because I knew then that my life, like everyone's, meant something. I knew one day my life would become better. I just didn't know how. I must have believed when I was seventeen that it would be me and Jack and we would do it together, but we were two completely different people, on two totally different wavelengths. It was never going to happen no matter how hard I tried.

Before long the relationship between myself and Mick grew on every level and with very little effort, we got on so very well. I was still struggling with my self-belief but the more I reminded myself what I had learnt from reading 'Love Life, Live Life', the easier it was to accept that this was the right way forward. I was so overwhelmed with happy emotions that one random day I said to Mick, "I have something I want to tell you, I think I'm falling in love with you". He smiled and said, "I think I'm falling in love with you too". He has told me he loves me several times a day ever since that day, I tell him the same too.

I had never in my life experienced the amount of positive emotions I was feeling. I was the happiest I'd ever been, any negativity faded from my life and I felt so optimistic about the future. I was constantly smiling from ear to ear, listening to happy love songs, it was a feeling of pure bliss.

Mick and I took it up a level and started getting intimate. I was so nervous, and I told him that I was, he made me feel at ease and completely comfortable. I knew we weren't doing anything wrong but as someone who has been under the control of someone else for such a long time it took a while to adjust.

I hadn't taken any contraception for a long time as I hadn't needed to, and I made him aware of this and told him I would get it sorted. We hadn't been together long and more children was the furthest thing from my mind. But in a moment where it really mattered, he forgot this minor detail. We were in the living room, and it happened right on the 'doof doof' of a well-known soap! What had we just done?

Growing up with some Catholic fundamentals and having lost a child, abortion for me was a complete no. I had to face the reality that I could be pregnant with a man I hadn't long been seeing. He had got through thirty-eight years of his life with no children and yet five minutes with me and boom, pregnancy scare.

It wasn't long before I was feeling the effects, turns out his little swimmers went for it and made the finish line. I went to buy a test from a local supermarket and hoped and prayed that I wouldn't bump into anyone I knew, I even bought other things I didn't need so I could conceal the test within the basket of shopping.

Mick was at his home fifteen miles away at the time, but I had made him aware of what I was doing, he was patiently waiting for my call. As soon as I got home, I went upstairs to the bathroom to do the pregnancy test. Very quickly appeared a definite positive result. I needed to tell Mick, so I picked up my phone, I was so nervous. "Erm, I did the test and I am pregnant" I didn't know what else to say, he was silent. I don't think he realised his sperm worked. "Okay, we'll deal with it". What on earth did he mean by that? "I'll pop round and see you later so we can talk".

What had we done? Things had been going so well but I felt terrible again. There was no way I could even contemplate a termination. If it came to it I would bring this baby up alone with Toby and John. But Mick knew what he was doing. I had only recently met his parents, what would they think? Argh what a mess!

Mick came round after I put the boys to bed, he questioned whether I would think about aborting the pregnancy, but I refused and explained my reasoning behind my decision. He then used Jack as an excuse, saying it would cause a lot of problems, but Jack had moved on so that really wasn't an issue. Maybe Mick was scared? We didn't know each other well enough to have a child, did we?

I had been coping really well with the boys, I just knew either way I could and would do it. It was up to him if he wanted to stick around or not. We had arranged to go and have dinner at his parents' house, he told me not to mention anything to do with the pregnancy, I wouldn't have anyway, it was up to him to tell them. His parents, Pat and Roy, made me feel so welcome, they treated Toby and John as if they were their own grandchildren. Mick just needed some time to think about everything, I knew he would be an amazing dad and his parents' fabulous grandparents.

The sickness from this pregnancy was extreme and I was feeling incredibly tired. I would take the boys to school and sleep the day away. Mick had gone a bit quiet on me, usually throughout the day I would get a phone call or texts, but since I had found out I was pregnant things were not feeling the same. I hoped that everything would work out soon.

Mick knew I was feeling upset, after a few days he apologised and said he just needed to get things straight in his head. He told me he wanted to be with me more than anything and that he wanted to be a father to our baby. He told me that he would tell his parents about the pregnancy. From that day on he stayed with me continuously. He told his parents that they would soon be grandparents. It was from that point that life really started to change.

The sickness and tiredness only lasted for a few weeks and I soon began to feel much better. The date of the twelve week scan came. I couldn't believe I was back having baby scans, it had been four years since John. Everything looked good, all the measurements were right and the due date was within days of Imogen's due date. I was almost retracing exact steps from seven years ago to the day.

Mick would go to work at the garage during the day and always came back to me after work. He was incredibly supportive. Mick told his parents so I was aware that they knew I was expecting. He told me they were delighted with the news. They continued treating Toby and John as though they were their own grandchildren, which made me so happy. They hadn't had that in grandparents before. I hoped we would be one of those close families who saw each other all the time and looked out for each other. The type of family I'd wished for when I was a child.

We started buying beautiful baby bits but I desperately wanted to know the gender. We booked a private 4D scan for when the baby was fourteen weeks gestation. What a lovely Christmas present that would be.

On the morning of the 4D scan I was filled with feelings of anticipation and excitement. I remembered so visibly John's 4D scan and what an amazing experience it had been, I was excited to do it again. We made our way there and went straight in for our appointment. Again it was explained that this was in no way a medical examination. I lay on the couch eagerly awaiting the moment to come which would inform us of the baby's gender. On the screen was an image of this gorgeous little face, with a striking resemblance to John. It was almost like I had gone back in time, seeing his beautiful little face and I instantly made the assumption that we were expecting a little boy. "Would you like to know the gender of the baby?. "Yes please!", I said in excitement. "You're having a baby girl". Oh my! The rush of emotions from hearing those words. "Are you absolutely sure?". "Yes, she is definitely a girl". What an amazing moment, I was absolutely convinced otherwise, I could've cried in that moment, I'm surprised I didn't. We were both absolutely delighted beyond words. She finished what she was doing and we went to get the photos, so vividly clear of our beautiful unborn little girl. We went back to the car and I had to take a few moments to gather my thoughts. "Are you happy?" asked Mick. "I am more than happy, I can't believe we're having a little girl!".

We had been sitting in our car in the car park for some time and were really close to a large shopping centre. I couldn't wait to go and buy our daughter her first little outfit so we decided to go and buy one there and then. It was so much easier buying baby stuff when you knew what gender you were having. I'd bought so many boys clothes before, it was lovely looking through all the baby girl clothes. So many pretty little outfits, I could have bought them all! I was walking around the shop with the biggest smile on my face, absolutely delighted with the news we'd just received.

Mick could not wait to let his parents know our news, his mum was patiently waiting for a phone call. He rang her, "it's a girl mum, you're going to be nanny to a granddaughter!". "That is wonderful news, I'm so happy for you both!". They were both absolutely thrilled. Our baby would be the first biological grandchild to them and they longed for a girl in the family. Everything was just falling into place, everything was beginning to feel like it was meant to be.

Chapter 13: Complete

December 2014

It was almost Christmas, and it was going to be mine and Mick's first one together. It had always been a stressful time of the year for me, work was extra busy in December and there was always so much more to do at home. This year was already feeling completely different, I was beginning to feel the weight of the world being slowly lifted from my shoulders. Mick's parents invited us to spend Christmas Day with them. It was the first time I had ever really looked forward to the day. I had already had the best gift I could ever receive, which was knowing we would soon have our own daughter in our lives.

On Christmas Day when the boys got up, they were so excited to open their presents. They were thoroughly spoilt. They had brand new little Christmas Day outfits to wear, I loved to dress them the same as each other. They always looked so cute but I'm sure they will question me on that when they are older, especially John! According to him I'm rather embarrassing.

After we'd opened our gifts we got ourselves ready to head over to Mick's parents. They had gone to a lot of effort for us, it really was feeling more special than it had ever been before. They had a tree which was decorated so beautifully, covered in exquisite decorations, it shone as though it were covered in diamonds. Pat had spent a lot of time preparing the Christmas dinner. It was such a nice atmosphere to be in, they were so welcoming and made me and the children feel really comfortable in their company. It was everything I had ever wanted. I looked at my children with the biggest smiles on their faces, I just knew they were having a really nice time too. This was what family should be, this is the family I'd always dreamt to be a part of.

After dinner we were sitting in the lounge talking amongst ourselves and Mick came over to me and handed me a little gift bag, "happy Christmas Marley", he said as he passed me the gift. I wasn't expecting anything else, it completely caught me by surprise. It was so rare for me to be treated with such kindness I didn't know how to respond, it was a surreal feeling, I couldn't believe it was happening to me.

I opened up the bag and inside was a little box from a jeweller, I opened the box to a beautiful white gold necklace with a heart shaped pendant, there was a tiny little diamond within the heart. It was truly beautiful. "Mick, it is gorgeous, thank you so much". I was blown away by his gift, it made the gifts I bought him look a bit rubbish. He said "would you like me to put it on for you?". "Yes please". He carefully removed the necklace from its box, I turned my back to him and held my hair up so he could do the clasp up. "I can't do it, mum come and do this necklace up for me!". Bless him, at least he tried. I went over to Pat and she put the necklace on for me. I had never had such a beautiful item of jewellery, all these things I was experiencing were a world apart from the life I had been accustomed too. I kept reminding myself that I was good enough, to just enjoy it and be grateful that good things were happening to me.

The most perfect Christmas Day came to an end, the boys were getting tired and it was getting rather late. We thanked Pat and Roy for everything they had done for us, it really was the best Christmas of my life. Whilst we were driving home I reflected on the day we had just had, I was feeling so content, everything felt right and like it was meant to be. Thinking back to a year ago, my life was now entirely different, it was hard to believe how much had changed in such a very small space of time. We enjoyed a lovely Christmas week together. New Year's Eve was just us, at home. New Year brought fresh new beginnings and we had so much to look forward too.

I was due to have the final twenty-week scan, this was going to be my last. We went to the maternity unit and sat in the waiting room for our turn. I was feeling so happy, this pregnancy was going so well and we were already at the halfway point. The scan went really well, everything was absolutely fine. The next time we would see our little one she would be in our arms, I couldn't wait for that day to come.

In order of my pregnancies, my first, as you know, was a traumatic birth. My second was considered high risk due to the first. My third was considered normal, however it was still requested I was in hospital for the birth. However, during one of the antenatal appointments for my fourth pregnancy, the midwife suggested a home birth. I had never even known this was an option, so it wasn't something I had ever considered. How amazing would it be to have a home birth, after learning more about it I was adamant that was what I wanted.

Mick and I discussed the option of a home birth at great length, I was eager to do it, but he was quite apprehensive about the idea. He had never been present at any childbirth before so was understandably nervous at the thought of it. I managed to talk him round and as long as I was happy with the idea of it that's what mattered the most to him.

I had never brought my first daughter home from hospital. This setting to give birth would be the complete opposite scenario to Imogen. I wasn't going to have the opportunity again. It was explained to me that because the local hospital didn't have much in the way of extra facilities, giving birth at home was really not much different to giving birth there. When the time came the midwife would bring with her all that I would need, so ultimately I would have the exact same at home as I would of had if I was in the hospital. I was told that when labour began I was to ring the triage and let them know, then when the contractions got closer I would need to call again and request a midwife. It all had to be planned in advance, you couldn't just say at the last minute you would like a home birth. On my next antenatal appointment I let them know that we had made the decision to do it. I was so incredibly excited!

I left work for maternity leave in March. Within the two months we had left before the birth of our daughter in May, I nested and made sure we had everything we would need for our new arrival. We bought a beautiful pram and a new Moses basket. I put the basket up in our bedroom the same day, imagining that soon, my little girl would be laying in it. We had to start again from scratch as I no longer had the baby stuff from when the boys were babies. We bought clothes, nappies, everything we needed. I packed a hospital bag just in case it would be needed. We were ready for her arrival.

Mick was working every day at the garage and I was taking the children backwards and forwards to school and trying to get as much rest as I possibly could before our daughter arrived.

A few people in town had changed their attitude towards me, the school run sometimes felt a bit awkward especially as I was now obviously expecting another child. A lot of them had taken Jack's side and thought bad of me because I had moved on and was pregnant. It got to me, especially when 'friends' were liking his posts on social media and not mine. It probably sounds really silly. No one really knew the truth, very few people knew what had really happened when I was in London or knew I had left there with nothing to come home to because I no longer even had a home. They didn't know he was messaging other women. They didn't know I was still, even now, paying off the expenses for a funeral and Imogen still didn't have a headstone. They didn't know how much he had mentally abused me. They didn't know about how controlling he had been. They didn't know he had thrown me across rooms and held me up against walls. They didn't know we hadn't shared the same room in years or that he never once attended any appointment regarding Toby's disability and hadn't helped with getting the children in to school. It really got me down at times, but I wasn't going to broadcast the truth, I'd let them believe what they wanted to believe. I knew the truth and ultimately that's all that mattered. I'm sure if anyone of those people had been living like I had been they would understand.

I felt like I needed, and wanted, a complete fresh start away from everything, a new town where no one knew me. I needed to talk to Mick about this, but first, I have a baby to give birth to, it could wait for a while.

At around 6pm on 18th May 2015, my labour started. My mum had recently moved back to the UK from Geneva and was now living forty miles away. I called her as I thought it might be nice for her to be there as she had previously said she would like to be. I told her my labour had started and without a second thought she made her way over to me.

Mick was very relaxed over the situation, I didn't know how he would be but I was pleasantly surprised. Mum arrived and Mick said he was going to bed as he knew it was going to be a long night, alright for some hey! I was only seven days early from the due date so everything was safe to proceed with the labour at home. Of course by now I was what you might refer to as a pro when it came to having children, I could read all the signs well. This was now my fourth time giving birth.

By 12pm my contractions were really beginning to strengthen so I rang the triage and they sent a midwife to my home address. What an experience it was, I had gas and air when I needed it but I was also drinking cups of tea and watching comedy films! At 3am I thought Mick had milked it enough and went upstairs to him, I told him to get downstairs before he missed the birth of his daughter. He really didn't want to get up, I had awoken him from a deep sleep. I don't think he believed it was really happening as I was coping with the labour so well. I felt very calm and relaxed and really grateful I had this opportunity. I didn't personally know anyone else who had given birth at home. The midwife made a comment about how easy I was making it look.

About 4am another midwife came as I was clearly getting closer to giving birth, they were sat at the dining room end of the lounge having a chat between themselves. Mum was sitting on the armchair constantly asking me if I needed anything and keeping everyone topped up with their drinks of tea. Mick had finally made it downstairs and was sitting on the sofa and I was on my knees on the floor facing him, leaning on him for support. He really was as cool as a cucumber, holding my hands helping through every contraction. He kept saying how proud he was of me and how much he loved me, the soppy sod, it was lovely.

So, there we all were in the lounge, in pretty much the same spot as our little 'doof doof' was conceived. I suddenly felt our baby girl drop; I knew we would be meeting her any minute. I said to the midwifes "she's coming!", they looked at me and smiled as if to say I had a bit more time yet. Within that moment and one almighty pain and push, whilst still on my knees out popped our baby, like a bowling ball and she slid a short distance on the plastic mat the midwife had put down to protect the carpet. There before us was our beautiful daughter. Stunned at the sight that lay before us, Mick and I looked at each other and said simultaneously, "she's ginger!".

The midwifes rushed over and told me to pick up the baby, you would have thought that would have been the first instinct and not commenting on the colour of her hair, she definitely inherited that from his family! I gently picked her up and cradled her in my arms, she was absolutely beautiful.

Mick couldn't wait and called his mum, "you're a nanny". He cried and she cried with pure happiness. It was a beautiful moment. The entire experience went exceptionally well. I was very lucky. The midwifes did their checks and within ninety minutes of giving birth, we were left at home with our baby girl. It was the perfect way to end my days of ever being pregnant again. I was definitely done with all of that now and I felt, as I still do now, extremely fortunate and grateful that I was the mother to three very beautiful children.

The date was 19th May, which rather coincidentally, was the same due date as Imogen Lily, seven years earlier.

I soon got showered and dressed, feeling amazingly good about how well the home birth went. I was beyond pleased we had made that decision. It was without a shadow of a doubt the best decision we could have made. The boys had slept through the entire labour, so they would be waking up to a world different from the one they had when they went to bed the night before, they now had a new baby sister.

At 7:30am, mum went upstairs to wake up Toby and John, it was still a school day after all and they weren't getting the day off just because I'd just had a baby. Mum told them there was someone downstairs waiting to meet them. They came excited as to who it could be, they hadn't even expected to wake up with nanny in the house. The boys came into the lounge and looked around the room, what had nanny meant, they couldn't see anyone there to meet them.

I turned to the boy's and said, "good morning boys, look who came last night", as I said this, I was pointing towards the little Moses basket in front of me. I can't imagine what went through their minds at that moment, they slowly walked towards me and lovingly looked into the basket, "meet your new baby sister, Lacey". I had never seen two little faces light up in the way theirs did, their eyes widened, and they had smiles from cheek to cheek. It was truly magical. "Hello Lacey", said Toby. "How did you get here?". Bless him, he didn't understand that she couldn't talk. They both came over to me and gave me the biggest cuddle. "Love you mummy". My heart just melted. My little family now felt very complete. My beautiful boys and my gorgeous baby girl. My wonderful other half. This is truly what happiness is.

I took the boys back upstairs to get them ready, they had their breakfast and then mum walked them in to school for us. We were all by now feeling incredibly tired. Mum and Mick had a power nap on the sofas in the lounge, I left Lacey with them and went to bed for a couple of hours sleep. There wasn't much time to rest, not that we could sleep for long. A new baby is always a really exciting time. Pat, Mick's mum couldn't wait to come over and meet her granddaughter. She arrived just after 12pm, Mick placed Lacey in to her arms and you could just see the pure love radiating through her eyes. She looked so lovingly towards her, like she had just been given the greatest gift she had ever been given. It was such a special moment between them and the beginning of the most precious bond.

Pat brought with her the most beautiful card and bouquet of flowers. It was truly a significant moment in her life and it made me so happy. Mum went home shortly after as she was feeling extremely tired, but I really appreciated the effort she had gone to and everything she had just done for us. Pat stayed a little longer, she just couldn't put Lacey down, she was already very deeply in love with her.

After Pat left, Mick went to pick the two boys up from school, it was now just us five. My precious, beautiful little family. A happy, content and very loving environment. Everything I had ever wanted for my children.

I soon got into a good routine of school runs and taking care of our newborn. Life was pure bliss, everything was perfect, apart from one thing. I couldn't go anywhere in that town without seeing someone who I felt had stabbed me in the back or who reminded me of a bad memory. After all, it was only a very small town. I was still feeling like we needed a fresh start somewhere new, but not too far away, I still wanted to see Marley and Imogen was buried there. I couldn't ever go too far from her.

I spoke to Mick about how I was feeling, and he could see without too much explanation that it was a good idea. Although Mick was always with me, he still had his own place fifteen miles away. His place wouldn't have been suitable for a family of five, he had a residential caravan, it could never have been a family home. It was fine as a home when it was just him. I also felt there was a lot more for the children in the town he lived opposed to where I lived. I imagined that if we lived there, they would have a wonderful childhood with lots to do right on our doorstep.

Mick suggested he would buy us a house and we could make a complete fresh start. We found a house which was cheaply priced for what it was but it did require a lot of work. I could see past the existing dated interior of the house and it would definitely work for our little family. It was situated in a quiet cul-de-sac. Mick put in an offer which was accepted almost instantly. It was so exciting I'd never before lived in a house we could call our own. I'd never had the opportunity to put my stamp on a house, I had so many ideas.

Now all I had to do was sort out the house I was living in, there was a lot to do but all the work was going to be worth it. Since my mum began renting the house things had been accumulating, the loft still had many of my family's belongings. Every weekend we emptied more and more stuff, chipping away at each room one by one. We were barely taking any of the old furniture and belongings with us and literally starting again from scratch. We bought new furniture for the boys' bedroom, some gorgeous baby furniture for Lacey's room. We bought a new bed, never in my life had I slept on a brand-new bed and mattress.

The house purchase completed in the August and we hired tradesmen to do the work which was necessary with a target date of moving in during the October half term. I contacted the local council and arranged new school places for the boys, everything was easily falling into place. Life was quite literally flowing.

Jack was living in Norfolk with his girlfriend and her three kids but was looking into moving them into the area. Because we were now moving out, I suggested he speak to the landlord about taking over the tenancy. Everything had always been in my name, never his. Jack did exactly that and when we were ready to move out, they would be moving in.

The new house was revamped from top to bottom, it was beautiful and I couldn't wait to move in and begin a fresh new chapter of our lives.

The boys had their last day at their school, we said goodbye to our friends, and we left to go and start our new life as a family. The move was only fifteen miles away so we weren't going too far. It would also be the first time I would be living in the same town as the company I worked for, our new house was literally around the corner from work. It instantly felt like home, it was such a nice environment to be in. We settled into our new way of life easily, everything was feeling 100% right.

Chapter 14: Changes

October 2015

The move went well and we settled into our new home and town. John was in reception year at school, so technically it was his first official year of school. He had his start date the first day back after October half term. However, things were slightly more complicated regarding Toby. He had a place at his new school, but they were not ready for him to start, they were trying to source a one-to-one assistant for him. He had to stay with me at home. The school was an infant school where children stayed until the end of year two and then moved to a junior school. Toby was in year two, so in his final year of infants. It was proving difficult for the school to find someone suitable as Toby would only be attending the school for the rest of that school year.

I was growing increasingly concerned with the lack of communication regarding a start date for Toby. It was incredibly frustrating. I had everything ready for him to go, his school uniform was just waiting to be worn. But I heard nothing. He was off school for weeks. Eventually the school did contact me saying they had employed a new member of staff for Toby and he was given a start date for the first day of spring term, after Christmas.

We were now living close to Mick's parents, which was lovely as we would very regularly pop in to see them. We had a life I had always dreamed off. A happy family home with love and laughter and grandparents close by for the children. We all grew very close and became a strong support network for each other, we were, in my opinion, a real functional family.

Mick's parents had told us about a holiday resort which is on the Norfolk coast, they made it sound like a great place to go, showing us videos online of what the resort offered. "The children would really enjoy it there, there is so much for the children to do, it's unlike anywhere else you have ever been". They then suggested we book the Christmas break and spend our Christmas there, all of us together. No cooking or cleaning, no stress. It certainly sounded fantastic. I didn't know you could even go away over Christmas, to be honest I'd never even thought about it. It sounded like a great idea and I was really excited, I couldn't wait to experience everything they had been telling us about. We hadn't been on holiday for a while and in all honesty, I hadn't been on many holidays at all.

John had a fantastic first half term at his new school, he was making friends and getting on well in class. I had no concerns regarding Toby starting at the same school after the holidays. On the last day of term, I picked John up and instantly all our focus then turned to our upcoming Christmas getaway. As always, I had so much to get organised. I needed to hand out all the presents to my family members, sort out which gifts we would be taking with us and which we would leave for when we got back, we just didn't have the room in the car to take it all. I had to pack the suitcases and make sure I had everything Lacey would need. She was only seven months old, so I needed to take a lot of baby stuff. It was actually pretty stressful getting everything ready, but on the evening of 22nd December, everything was ready with the car packed to the brim. Christmas began, all the hard work was done.

The following morning, with the car ready to go, all we had to do was get ourselves and the children ready. They were filled with absolute excitement, I loved seeing them so happy. We were about to have the most amazing Christmas together and it was little Lacey's first Christmas. We first drove to Mikes parents as we had planned to follow them to the resort. The drive took a little under two hours so wasn't too far from home.

As we drove through the entrance of the resort we were stopped and greeted by the one and only Father Christmas sitting on his slay, the children thought it was the most spectacular sight they had ever seen. Listening to them discussing their amazement at who they had just seen simply melted my heart. We drove around the grounds and parked at one of the many car parks available to us. It looked unlike any place I had been before and we hadn't even got into our accommodation yet. From the outside it looked like one huge hotel, I could see a golf course and a field. I thought how lovely it would be there in the summer months.

Pat and Roy already knew their way around, so we left the car still packed and followed them to the reception area. Grandad Roy held each of the boys by their hand and asked them if they were excited. They looked back at him, wide eyed with the biggest smiles, nodding quickly at him whilst saying yes in such an excited manor. They were in their element. Within a few minutes we reached the reception area which was filled with the aromas of mulled wine and mince pies. Mick and Roy headed over to reception to check us all in, calling us one by one to have our resort wristbands put on. There were entertainment staff greeting all the children and issuing each one with a resort passport which contained activities for them to do. Already I was seeing signs that this really was a great place for all the family to enjoy. Beside the staff organising the children were more staff handing out little sausages coated in honey and sesame seeds, mince pies, warm freshly baked cheese twists, hot chocolate and mulled wine. Both Pat and I were given a big box of chocolates as a welcome gift. I was already blown away and couldn't wait to see what the Christmas break would have in store for us.

We soon found our accommodation which was a bungalow and was also very close to the main venue. Pat and Roy were booked into the hotel, the rooms were very luxurious. Mick went to get the luggage out from the car and whilst he was gone there was a knock on the door. I opened it to two elves with gifts of colouring books, sweets and chocolates for the children. I sat on the bed and just took it all in, watching my children already having such a wonderful time. How had we got here? I seriously feel incredibly lucky to be having this experience and to be seeing my children so happy too, I can't even put into words how I was feeling in that very moment.

Once we had unpacked, we decided to have a walk around and familiarise ourselves with the resort. Everything in sight was perfectly placed, the Christmas decorations were absolutely beautiful. I was quite literally mind blown. Everyone we saw was full of joy and pure happiness. It was known to be one of the best breaks of the year at the resort and getting booked in could sometimes prove to be tricky, I was so pleased that we were there.

That evening we went into the most gorgeous dining room I had ever seen, we had our own waiter and the table we had was ours for the duration of the break. We had a three-course menu for every lunch and dinner. Breakfast was literally everything you could imagine, from fruit, cereal, toast, croissants, full continental to full English. The children could either order from the menu or visit the buffets and choose from lots of children's favourite foods.

The evening entertainment was set in a modern theatre with layered seating and a bar stretching from one side of the room to the other. There was a buffet table with sweets, a chocolate fountain and cheese and biscuits, which I love. Everything was all within the cost of the break. You definitely wouldn't go hungry there. The entertainment was spectacular, not that I'd been to a West End show but I was told the shows were of similar quality and the comedy team, who were quite literally bonkers, were absolutely hilarious. The main man host was first class, it was all absolutely fabulous. I really tried to take in all in and enjoy each and every single moment.

On our second day of the break, which was Christmas Eve, the children had the most perfect day from the moment they woke up until they went to bed. They met Santa's reindeer's, played in a giant inflatable snow globe, went on go-karts, a bouncy castle and a huge inflatable obstacle course. There was just so much for them to do. Throughout all of it we piled on the pounds, we had so much food.

That evening, we were sitting in the theatre of the resort, I was dressed up like I had never dressed up before, everyone looked so glamorous. The bar on Christmas Eve was free and everyone was having a truly very merry time! As showtime began I heard my name coming through the speakers. I looked up to see my name on the big screens. I wondered what was going on. I instantly turned to look at Mick, wondering what he had done. "Marley, someone has a question for you", "What me?", I said as I looked at the host, pointing at myself. "Yes, you, but who is asking a question? It's Mick, Mick is asking the question". As I turned to look again at Mick, he presented me with a box which had a beautiful diamond ring glistening in it. The hosts put the microphone up to Mick and he said those four big words, "Will you marry me?". The words were not only coming from his mouth but were also written on the big screens. Mick was there in front of me with the host still holding the microphone to his mouth, there were seven hundred people in the room and all eyes were on me. The microphone was brought towards me, "Yes! Yes, I'll marry you". With that the host grabbed the ring off Mick, shouting down the microphone, "look at that, look at the size of that diamond" He started running around the theatre showing random members of the audience the engagement ring. He handed the ring back to Mick and he placed it on my ring finger. It fit perfectly. The host shouted, "she said yes. Congratulations to you both!".

What on earth had I done in my life to deserve this man, who was now my fiancé? For the remainder of the break we had people congratulating us and offering to buy us drinks, from the free bar. Just before midnight the entertainment team started a ten second countdown to Christmas, much like you would do at New Year. As the clock struck midnight party poppers went off everywhere, everyone was wishing each other a merry Christmas and we all danced the night away. It was the most magical night, truly unforgettable.

On Christmas Day I woke up early, Mick and the children were still soundly asleep. I reached over to the bedside cabinet and picked up the ring box, I carefully opened it and just gazed at my beautiful engagement ring. I took it from the box and gently placed it back on my finger and of course admired it some more. I had previously thought that things like this didn't happen to people like me, but it was all definitely happening, it was so good it really felt as though I was dreaming, I was really living the dream. I got out of bed and made myself a coffee, then one by one my sleeping beauties woke up. Merry Christmas mummy, I turned around and there was Toby, rubbing his eyes and still half asleep. "Come here babe", I gave him the biggest hug,

"Merry Christmas, I love you so much, we're going to have the best Christmas ever".

Christmas at the resort was completely different to how we had ever had Christmas at home. The first thing we had to do was get ready and head over to the restaurant for breakfast. The resort staff had put congratulations balloons at our table and we were still having people coming over and congratulating us. The atmosphere was electric with happiness and joy. After breakfast we all went to Pat and Roy's room, we had given them the presents and told the children Santa had dropped them off with them. Everyone opened their gifts and afterwards we went to the theatre. Father Christmas was there handing out presents to each and every child who was at the resort. The rest of the day was filled with activities of all sorts, we had a lovely Christmas dinner and again in the evening another amazing show.

On Boxing Day, we went swimming in the resorts pool, the water was lovely and warm. As I was pushing Lacey around in her baby float, she only fell asleep, it relaxed her so much. After swimming we went to one of the halls where there was an indoor Christmas Street market. It had games, popcorn and candy floss stalls and lots of entertainment with the comedy team. The break had been everything Mick's parents had said it would be. I had never had a Christmas like it, in fact I never knew Christmas could be like it. On the 27th we had to pack up and head home, but before we left, we booked for the following year, we couldn't wait to do it all again.

After returning home we had a week before the children went back to school. My attention turned back to work as my maternity leave was ending. The job wasn't the same anymore, the company had been taken over and gone were the incentives and the company balls. Long gone were the days where you were respected as an individual for your dedication and service to the company, it didn't feel like the same job anymore. When I first started my job, I was so grateful to Max for helping get a place within the company, but I had now completely lost all interest. Within two weeks of returning to work I had a conversation with Mick that I was going to hand my notice in. My manager and area manager tried talking me out of it, I had twelve years experience which was invaluable to them. My mind however was made up. Every shift I had I didn't even want to be there, although I still worked to a high standard. The irony of it all was that I had always driven at least thirty minutes each way to work, now living around the corner, I was quitting. Maybe I had just liked my little drive time.

I had to work my notice, every single shift just seemed to drag on, ten minutes would feel like sixty. On my last day it felt just like any day at work except this time I knew I wouldn't be going back. What had started as an amazing opportunity had turned completely flat. I had a quiet moment to myself and read through all the old emails I still had from Max, all the banter and the help he gave me during the course of my employment. It made me quite emotional reading them all. I missed my friend terribly and after that last day I would no longer have any access to those emails, so I photographed them. That might sound like a strange thing to do but that's what I did. I left work that day after all my years of service with not so much as a good-luck card, I knew for sure then that I had made the right decision. Mick was supportive in such a way that I didn't at that time have to work, instead I could fully focus on bringing up my three beautiful children. I really appreciated that my life provided me with the opportunity to do that and it was all because of Mick.

I really enjoyed taking the children to school and spending my time between our home and Micks parents home with Lacey. She would have a nap in the afternoon and instead of putting her down in the cot I would rather lay down on the sofa and cuddle her whilst she slept. Moments like those are so incredibly precious, children grow up so quickly and before you know it, they are all attending school. I wanted every moment to mean something.

I had always driven old cars, there is absolutely nothing wrong with that. The cars I'd had very rarely let me down and served the purpose I needed them for. I loved every car that I had ever owned and even gave each one a name. When I had read the book 'Love Life, Live Life', there was a part of which taught the technique of visualisation. I began to imagine the car I would like and imagines myself driving it. You must really see yourself driving the car and imagine your own hands holding onto the steering wheel. I did that at the time of reading the book, I had images in my mind of myself driving a big white Range Rover. I never once thought it was possible or that one day I would own one, I simply just enjoyed the thought of it. I never told anyone that I'd had these thoughts, it was just something I did personally.

I was then driving a little SUV, I had always liked the thought of owning a 4x4 and a couple of years before, one had come up at a price affordable to me. It had a few dents and scratches, but I loved how well it handled in all weathers, I felt I was safe and my children were safe in that car.

Mick said he thought it was about time we sold my car and got ourselves a bigger family car. It was a squeeze as it wasn't very big inside and because the boys needed booster seats and Lacey needed a car seat, we did need a car with more room. Mick had arranged to go and view a few cars, he was very particular about making sure that the car he bought ticked every box and it had to be absolutely immaculate.

After weeks of searching he finally found the one. He had gone with his dad as the car was a few hundred miles away. Late afternoon he returned with our new car. He walked into the house and asked me to go outside and have a look at it. I had no idea what car he had bought, but I didn't mind what it was. I knew whatever he had chosen would be perfect.

I put my shoes on and went to go out the front door but as soon as I looked at what was on our driveway I stopped in my tracks. I turned to Mike, "wow, that's not ours, is it?". "Yes, it is, do you like it?", "Like it? I love it! I've never driven anything as big as that, do you think I'll be okay driving it?". "You'll be fine", and he handed me the keys.

The car he had bought us was a Range Rover Vogue, in a beautiful Buckinghamshire Blue colour. I opened the door and sat in the driving seat. The interior was an almost white leather with black detailing. I put my hands on the steering wheel, it wasn't an image in my mind anymore, it was real. I'd never been in a Range Rover let alone driven one, I honestly didn't know if I could handle such a big car. This car was very large and a seven-seater vehicle. It was entirely different to anything I had ever driven before and it was an automatic, I had only ever driven a manual. It had TVs in the headrests, with real digital channels. It was eight years old, but it was definitely top of the range when it was new. I absolutely loved it and was completely overwhelmed. Mick encouraged me to learn how to drive it as soon as possible so I could break the comfort barrier I had. It drove like any other car, although it was a more luxurious drive. I had to get it into my mind how to drive an automatic car, Mick said it was easy, just don't use your left foot. Mick's parents offered to look after the children so Mick could help me with learning my way around the new car. I was so worried I'd damage it in some way, but he reassured me and said that even if anything did ever happen to it, ultimately, it was only a piece of metal. In my mind it was a lot more than that. I was used to driving my old cars and wasn't fussed if I curbed a wheel, I would have to be extra careful with this one.

We put the children's car seats in and Mick took us all for a drive around town in our new car, it was so exciting. I was trying to familiarise myself with where everything was. We took the children to Mick's parents and Pat came out to see it, she thought it was beautiful. Then we went to a local retail park with a large car park. The shops were all closed and so the car park was empty, it was the ideal opportunity for me to jump in the driver's seat. I adjusted the mirrors as Mick talked me through. Then I put the car into drive, I slowly lifted my foot of the break and without touching the accelerator the car began to move, I quickly put my foot back onto the break. "I forgot to mention that's what an automatic does when you take your foot off, it will move". Thanks Mick, now you tell me! I tried again, this time fully aware about how it worked, after one lap around the car park I drove towards the exit, "this is easy!". "I know and I knew you would be okay in it". I drove around town a couple of times and then headed back to Mick's parents. I couldn't believe I had just driven a Range Rover.

When we got to their house they asked how I had got on with it. I was so pleased to tell them that within minutes I felt completely comfortable behind the wheel. They were really pleased, especially now we had a car which fitted us all in perfectly. We stayed for a cup of tea and then took the kids home so we could put them to bed.

Life was just getting better and better all the time, we were all so blissfully happy as a family. It really was one good thing after another. I would often reflect on how life had been and how it was now. Wondering how my life had become the way it was now. I'd often think back to my own childhood and how different my children were growing up. They were not growing up broken but knowing they were deeply loved and nurtured to the absolute best of my abilities. Mick had become such an amazing father to them all and never once treated the boys any differently to Lacey. They were all treated equally the same, which is exactly how it should be.

We spent a lot of time with Mick's parents and it came up in conversation that it would be a good idea if we sold our home and they sold their home so we could buy a bigger house, big enough for us all. Mick's mum would be close to her grandchildren and watch them grow up, they would be there to help and support us in any way we needed and we, in turn, would be there for them. The thought of doing this seemed like a good idea. I remembered how I had longed to grow up close to my own nanna because I loved being in her company. I again had an opportunity to make sure my children had everything they could dream of in their own lives, to ensure they would have the best childhood they could have. It would be so different to my own circumstances, I had once been so vulnerable and alone and now I was rich in love and family. It was because of my memories, past thoughts and experiences that I agreed to the idea.

Mick didn't need any time to think about it, he had always had a very close relationship to his mum. I used to tell him all the time that he was so lucky to have parents like his, and how I hoped that when my children were older, I would love the same with them. It was incredibly important to me that my children knew that we would always be there for them, our door would always be open and our home would always be their safe place.

I may update this book in years to come and let you know how that went for me.

Toby played a huge part in the final decision. The idea was to have a self-contained annex for Pat and Roy so we would still have our own space. Because Toby had autism, he would unlikely be able to live independently as an adult. I would never put him into any situation that would make his life difficult so the annex could be given to him to live in when the time came. Toby could have his own space but we would always be there for him, to help with anything he needs. It all made so much sense.

We had only moved into our house very recently but because it was newly renovated it would be an easy sell. We had the work completed on the basis that we would be living there for quite some time, so it was quite sad we were already thinking of selling. After a lengthy discussion with Mick's parents, it was decided that we would go ahead with our plans. Both of our properties went on the market and we explained to potential buyers that the purchase was likely to take a considerable amount of time as it was based on two properties being sold.

We had several viewings very quickly after the house went onto the market. Even though the buyers were aware of the situation that it would take extra time to complete, a bidding war began on our house. We accepted the higher offer, but due to the bank valuing the property below the accepted purchase price, we had to lower what we had accepted to fall in line with the actual value. That was slightly disappointing but, we had sold. Mick's parents were not having as much luck as us. Meanwhile, we were hunting for a suitable house to meet our needs, nothing seemed to tick every box without needing a massive amount of work. We were viewing houses daily and were beginning to wonder if what we wanted was actually available within the budget. We discussed stopping altogether and taking both properties off the market. One afternoon we saw a lovely property appear on the house selling app, it was fresh onto the market, within budget and had all the potential that we required. We came to the realisation that we would have to create our exact vision ourselves but we wanted to have the majority of what we needed already in place. The house we found was big enough and half of the downstairs would easily convert into a self-contained annex. There were enough bedrooms for each of the children to have their own room, the garden was lovely and big, there was also a double garage which would make an ideal workshop for Roy. There was enough parking space for each of us, it was 100% the perfect house for us all. We arranged a viewing for that very evening, the first foot I stepped in I had this feeling of knowing that this was indeed our future home. It was perfect. Mick and Roy told the current homeowners that we would be putting an offer forward first thing in the morning for the full amount. It was all so very exciting. The offer was instantly accepted. As if by fate, a few days later, Pat and Roy had buyers for their property too. Again things were falling perfectly into place, life was definitely still flowing.

We started packing up our home, once again getting ready to move. I just wanted my children settled. Toby in particular wasn't very good at handling changes in his life and over the last year he'd already had so many changes. I knew deep down that once this was completed; we wouldn't be moving house again for a very long time and therefore what we were doing was worth it. We really didn't have much to pack up. Our home was very much to 'show home' standards and we were absolutely sure that the family that were buying it would certainly be happy with their purchase. After eight long weeks the house purchase completed, and we started moving our stuff over to the new house.

We had to share a kitchen initially as the annex conversion needed to be done. Within a few weeks our home was taken over by builders, every morning at 8am they came. It lasted weeks on end. It was extremely stressful whilst the work was being done, they were noisy, the carpets became filthy and everywhere became covered with a chalky dust. It just seemed to be never ending. Our relationships within the family became strained and we even began to regret the path we had taken. However the work did eventually complete, which was an absolute relief. We got through it together and calm within the family was restored.

Pat and Roy now had their own lounge, bedroom, kitchen and bathroom. They also had a conservatory built, that was all their own space. We had our own kitchen and lounge and the whole of the upstairs of the house. The children all had a room of their own, each with a double bed. It came together how we had all thought, and hoped, it would. The children loved having their grandparents so close, they spent time between the two sides of the house. The grandparents loved it too. We were also now living closer to the school than we had done. The school was now well within walking distance. Roy and Mick started to go to work together at the garage and Pat was around for company.

It's a really nice way to live. I don't think there is much, that is better in life than having and being a part of a close and loving family. I value and cherish them all.

Chapter 15: Happily Ever After

September 2016

Toby was going into year 3 and about to start the junior school. School wasn't going as well for him as it previously had. The older he was getting the more difficult life was becoming for him. The differences between Toby and the rest of his class were becoming increasingly apparent. He sat with his one-to-one at a desk the far end of the classroom, well away from the rest of his class. His back would be towards everyone else and he was never included. He was never able to participate in anything the rest of his class did. He was becoming more frustrated whilst at school and he would show his frustrations by screaming 'argh' as loud as he could.

Whether it was sports day or school plays, he was never included. I realised the choice I had made at the beginning of his school life was definitely the wrong one and I felt terrible about it. I needed a way to correct it for him and get him where he would have a better school life and with better opportunities for his future.

Every year children with an education and health care plan need to have the plan reviewed, it's a standard procedure that I had become very familiar with. During the review meeting you have the opportunity to state that the current placement for the child is no longer suitable. We stated this at the next review meeting and patiently waited for the new updated care plan to come back to us. When it did come back, the council could not change Toby's current placement and we had to start an appeal against that decision. Again, that is standard practice, it is extremely rare for the school placement to be amended just because it had been stated on the review. As with most things in life, there was a lengthy process to follow.

All the special educational needs schools in the area were substantially oversubscribed. We visited a special needs school, nine miles away and I just knew in my heart that was where Toby would be spending his school life, he just had to have a place there. They did so much for the children, they worked according to the curriculum whilst teaching vital life skills like shopping and cooking. If he could get a place within that particular school, he would be in a class with likeminded children like him, he would no longer be isolated. I knew how I'd felt during the times I had faced isolation in my life, I certainly did not want any of those feelings transferring over to my own children. I was trying to change my children's future by changing my own life. If I recognised any negative reoccurrences, I would, where possible, stop them in their tracks.

There were many meetings and letters written during the appeal. It was an incredibly stressful and grueling process. Even though, like I have said before, to me, in my eyes Toby was perfect as he was, these processes constantly highlight what is not 'right' with your child and it's a very negative and emotionally draining experience. As much as I wanted to shout from the rooftops how incredibly clever and gifted my son was, the focus was always on the things he was not capable of doing. There was no denying my sons disability, even strangers recognised his autistic traits, which in one way of looking at it, was a good thing. It shows that an awareness of his condition exists.

We had a court date set for October to go against the council to obtain a place for Toby. There were so many times I feared the worst and I really thought it wouldn't happen. I blamed myself and thought I had seriously let my precious son down. The boy who probably saved my life, just by being there. I fought for him with everything I had in me. I had to. It's such a shame that it is such a heartbreaking and draining process to go through.

Mick throughout the entirety of the process was an absolutely amazing support. He attended every single meeting, he went through all the paperwork with me. It was all just incredibly stressful but it would have been so much harder without him helping me though it. We were just trying to do the best for our son.

Two weeks before the court date an email pinged to my phone saying Toby was being offered a place at the special needs school which we had requested. It is quite simply the best place for him and I was incredibly grateful he got into that school.

Within a year I had resigned from my long-term employment, moved house again, started driving a Range Rover and Toby had gained a place at the best special needs school in the area. Life was becoming a dream come true and it all changed because I changed my mindset. All those wishes and dreams I'd had became my reality, one by one.

It was almost Christmas again and we set off for another amazing break at the resort in Norfolk. While we were there, our attention was drawn to that fact it had been a year since our engagement. We decided that in the new year, we'd set a date and make plans to get married. We just hadn't had the chance to focus on our wedding until then. We started talking about booking a venue. I definitely didn't want a big church wedding and neither did Mick, it just wasn't for us. We were looking through an online selling platform and we came across a deal for a wedding package at a highly discounted price. We were both keen on the idea of getting married at this particular venue so gave them a call to arrange a visit and discuss the deal we were looking at. It was a very comprehensive package which was being offered, it included the service, food, a party, DJ, a buffet and accommodation. It had pretty much everything covered. It was at a hotel with fairly nice grounds and we decided it would be perfect for us. We let them know there and then that we would like to book our wedding, but we had to have the deal that we had found online. It wasn't a problem at all for them to sort it all out for us and the date was set for 20th August 2017. A lovely summer wedding, I was so excited, we had a date. A day we could all look forward too.

All those hours I had spent drawing wedding dresses as a child, that dream I'd had was also about to come true. Pat, Roy and my mum, all said they would cover the cost of the dress. I couldn't believe I was now in the position where I would be the one to try on beautiful dresses. I made an appointment at a local wedding dress boutique and Pat, my mum and Marley all accompanied me to help me choose. I felt again like it was all a wonderful dream, I was feeling so incredibly lucky.

I tried a few different dresses on and as beautiful as each one of them was, I hadn't found the one. I thought because we were getting married in a hotel I should keep the dress a bit simpler. Then I saw one, closely resembling the style of the dress I used to draw. I put the dress on, walked out of the changing room to where my family and Marley were sitting and they all gasped. Pat cried and Marley had tears in her eyes. Marley then said, "you look absolutely beautiful, that is the one". I felt incredible in this dress, it was absolutely stunning. I hadn't even thought to ask how much it was. Then I realised I better ask, it turned out to be a lot of money, I felt that it was just too much. Pat insisted we order that dress, I would only get this opportunity once, so it had to be perfect. I cried, I was so happy, Marley took a photo of me on my phone and over the months I kept going back to the photo just to look at it, in disbelief that it was me in the picture. I still couldn't believe that this was all happening for me.

When Marley and I were children, we used to talk about getting married one day and made a promise to each other that if we did, we would be each other's maid of honour. Remembering my promise to her, I asked her if she would be. Without hesitation she said yes. I didn't want any other bridesmaids, just Marley, she was the one person who, throughout everything, had been there constantly. I bought Marley a beautiful navy bridesmaid dress, navy was our colour scheme. I also bought her some lovely shoes, a little bag, earrings, necklace and a watch. I wanted her to know how much I appreciated her, and I hoped she would feel on the day as fabulous as I did. I booked us both to have our hair and make-up done professionally on the day too. Something which neither of us had ever experienced.

Toby and John had little matching suits to Mick's suit and Lacey had a gorgeous white dress to match mummy's, she had a cute little navy ribbon around the waist. My heart melted with the sight of all my children on my wedding day. My heart was full, and I felt so proud of them.

We paid extra to have the reception room decorated beautifully, all the chairs were covered in white and had navy sashes, the walls were all draped in white. The tables were set so exquisitely. There was so much that had to be organised even though our wedding package was so good.

From a young age I never believed my life would ever become what it had. I never thought I would even get married, all that stuff happened to other people, it happened to normal people. I had never felt like a normal person throughout my entire life. All my childhood dreams had vanished along the way. Strangely, all my dreams were coming back to me, although hidden dreams, they were always there the entire time.

We spent months planning our special day, getting every last detail exactly how we wanted it. We booked to stay at the hotel the night before the wedding, Marley and her family were coming the day before too. It was lovely having that time with her and I was so incredibly happy she would be spending this very special day with me, it truly meant the world to me.

I barely slept the night before the wedding. The hotel was quite noisy and you could hear people walking the corridors though the night. Marley and I were booked in at 9am for our hair and makeup. I had little Lacey booked for her hair to be done too. The beauty salon was on the hotel premises which was ideal. I hadn't shared a room with Mick as that would've been bad luck and we were very careful walking around the hotel to make sure we didn't bump into him. Invited guests were slowly turning up, it was so incredibly nerve wracking but also at the same time it was very exciting.

After breakfast we went to the salon, Marley had her hair done first whilst I was having my makeup done. Whilst we were there the photographer had arrived and was taking photos. Me and Marley swapped and I had my hair done while Marley had her makeup done. She looked absolutely stunning. Then it was little Lacey's turn, she looked so small sitting in the hairdressers chair, she had her hair styled into these gorgeous little curls, she looked absolutely beautiful. My little princess. We went back to the room and were asked to go to the honeymoon suite to get ready in. There were chocolates and champagne. My dress was already there, hanging off the curtain pole. The sun was shining directly onto it, it looked absolutely stunning. Mick had left a gift in my room in a fairly large jewellery box. I opened it and inside was the most amazing diamond necklace, it was breathtaking. I couldn't believe what I had just received. I had only bought him a set of cuff links.

In all my wisdom, I asked my dad to walk me down the aisle. I hadn't had a lot to do with him for such a long time but it seemed like the right and traditional thing to do. As I walked down the aisle we had a singer from our favourite resort singing the song 'a thousand years', he has the most fabulous voice, the moment was quite simply perfect. I was locked in arms with my dad, dressed in my beautiful white wedding dress and holding my bouquet consisting of white and navy blue flowers with a charm holding a photo of Imogen, all of my children were with me that day.

When I got to the end of the aisle, dad, Marley and Lacey all took their seats. I stood side by side with Mick, the absolute love of my life. He was almost in tears of happiness but held it together well. I was so nervous, I don't think I had ever, until then, spoken out loud in a room full of people. I managed to say my vows, out loud, in front of all of our friends and family. I felt the most intense happiness and love I had ever felt, standing in a room full of people who were watching on with happy tears in their eyes. My beautiful little boy John had the rings on a little white silk cushion, I took Mick's ring and placed it on his finger, Mick placed my ring on my finger, "I now pronounce you husband and wife".

This was the happiest moment of my life, I'd just married my best friend, my soul mate, my everything. I had a husband and I was his wife. My children were so happy and content. We disappeared for a while to have photos taken and then headed back to the venue for food and speeches. We thanked everyone for joining us on our special day, it meant the world to us both. We had group photos taken and then it was time to party. It was the best wedding party and it was our wedding party. It was the most epic wedding of all time and we wouldn't have done one thing differently. Not long after our wedding myself and Mick jetted off for a week in Mexico to a five-star resort, it was heaven on earth. Never before had I'd been anywhere where the resorts staff would come into the sea and bring you drinks! I fell in love with the sunrise off the Mexican Caribbean coast. It was a wonderful honeymoon, full of amazing memories I would never forget.

Before long it was back to reality, but not for long. It was soon Christmas again and of course we spent it at the resort in Norfolk. Lacey still didn't know what a Christmas at home felt like. She was now at the age where she was able to start nursery and before we knew it we were dropping her off for her first day.

In what felt like a very short amount of time, all my children were in an education setting and I needed a job or something to do with my time. I had worked since I was fourteen and not working just wasn't for me. I thought back to the time I worked in the salon and remembered I had missed out on the opportunity to learn the trade, all because I had to stop as I needed a job where I could earn enough money to support myself. On deeper thought I had never even wanted to do hairdressing; I had only worked in a salon as a teenager because my parents made me get a job.

I knew that I was creative, I had always liked doing my own nails, so I decided to enrol on a training course to learn to become a nail technician. I didn't take to it easily, it was certainly a lot harder than I had ever given anyone credit for. I learnt many aspects of the trade, including how to do manicures, gel polish nails, acrylic nails, nail art. You name it, I learnt it. I soon realised though that salon work wasn't really what I wanted. I enjoyed creating beautiful nails, but I wasn't feeling that it was where I belonged. I would have loved to have stayed in education and been able to naturally study what I was truly interested in but I didn't know what that was, I was deeply lost.

******

This is just my story so far and I am grateful you have let me share it with you and I have written all these words you have read from my memories which makes those words something very real. They have flowed from my mind into a written form and I have enjoyed almost every second of it. At some points it has, understandably, been an incredibly hard process. With doing this, particularly when writing about the more difficult times, it has left me with some of the worst headache's which I have ever experienced. Who knew that writing could both be physically and also quite mentally painful. However for the most part it does indeed feel like this has been a completely natural process, almost as though these words were meant to be written by me and I was indeed supposed to one day share this story with the world. This is me, this is exactly what I was naturally meant to become, I have never studied to become a writer but I do feel that I was meant to write. Ever since I was a young age, I had always imagined trying to find a way of helping others by using my own story. A story which highlights different points where things could have turned out differently and a way to help others see where they could also in turn recognise scenarios within their own life's, which would lead on to help them change their own course of life. Doing all of this for the greater good. I still can't believe that I have actually done it, I found the strength from somewhere inside of me, to accomplish one of the greatest goals and dreams which

I have ever had. I am understandably scared to set these words free and forward them on to others to read. Wondering if they will be received in the manner I intend, yet also wondering if these words will genuinely relate to anyone else, which as you know has always been one of the greatest struggles.

It's an incredibly difficult process to be able to pinpoint events in your life that changed your course. It's only when you stop and really think about it, that things start to be become blatantly obvious. After everything I have ever been through, I always knew that I had something to say and I hope this story brings hope to others who long to be living a different life from the one they are living today. Helping to impact the lives of their own families for generations to come.

Marley call's me the real-life Cinderella, she has been with me from a early age and she knows exactly how hard it's been. She always telling me how proud she is of me. She's convinced my book will be turned into a movie and that my story will help other people. Love ya Marley.

I have kept every promise I have ever made to my children even before they were born. Every promise that I made to them when I was still a child myself, I consider that both magical and incredible. Even I do not fully understand how that has happened, maybe what you wish for really does come true? You may remember very close to the beginning of this story, I spoke of my father going to Florida and taking my brother Tom? You will recall I said to myself as a child, if I had children I would take them all. Well, we have taken all of our children to Florida and I am now completely Disney obsessed. I have definitely passed the love onto Lacey. Every time we see an advert on the TV she points it out, "it's Disney mum, we have been there!". John wasn't much of a fan of the big rides, I even got escorted off one with him because it absolutely terrified him. Then there was Toby, he is a full-on adrenaline junky. I had read a tip online before we left that if you take anti travel sickness tablets, they stop you feeling unwell after you have been on a theme park ride, I was so glad I had read that piece of advice because it was true, it worked and I was able to take Toby on any ride he desired to try. He also spent his tenth birthday at Disney World. It really was everything, and more, that I had ever anticipated the experience to be. Another dream which certainly became reality and is now another beautiful memory.

You may have noticed that I have barely said a word regarding my dad, other than when I was growing up and when I had moved in with him briefly after I had lost the flat. I also mentioned him walking me down the aisle on my wedding day. You may or may not wonder what became of him? What kind of life would someone like him go on to live? Would he have a happy ending? Would he be spending his days with a close bond with his children and enjoying watching his grandchildren grow up? The answer to all of those questions is no. Dad has never stopped drinking. We very rarely see him as I really do not want my own children spending time with him and getting too familiar with him. He has had several new relationships with other women but not surprisingly, none of those new relationships have resulted in a happy ending for him. He ended up having a psychotic episode and was taken to hospital, this ultimately resulted with him being admitted to a mental health ward and he was sectioned for four months. His driving license was revoked and as a consequence he lost all methods of working that he had previously been able to do. He has lost everything and everyone who he had ever had in his life. He is now living on his own, in a bedsit with no family around him at all. You really do reap what you sow.

I would also like to let you know how it is working out for Toby and John with their father Jack. Generally everything is fine and we all get on well. We have had a few ups and downs throughout the years but most of the time things are ok in that respect. Jack does not support the boys financially but they do stay with him once a fortnight. So rather importantly he is there for them emotionally, which in my view is extremely important. Thankfully they were both so young when we separated that neither of them can remember a time when we had all lived together and I am extremely grateful for that. I am so glad that they don't remember any of the bad things that had happened inside the world I brought them in to. All they know and remember is the life they have now with me and Mick.

If I had stayed in a relationship with Jack, undoubtably they would have grown up in a toxic household just as I had as a child. Their reality is quite the contrary, they have a real childhood where they are allowed to be children. They are all growing up and developing into the people which they truly are without being repressed in any way, shape or form. Neither one of my children are similar, they all have a completely different character to each other. It is a huge joy and pleasure watching them all grow and I will look forward to seeing what they all become as grown-ups. Hopefully I am doing this parenting thing right, I suppose only time will tell.

Toby is happier and more settled in his school than he has ever been and he also has the potential to do very well with his life which brings me so much comfort. The support we now receive from the school is outstanding and I look towards Toby's future feeling much more relaxed and confident that he will just fine.

We must always treat our loved ones with kindness, respect and compassion, for we never know what curveball life with inevitably throw at us next.

Chapter 16: Right Choices

I have written in so much detail about the bad experiences in my life, that felt it was equally important to explain in some detail more of the most magical time's I have also experienced. I know only too well how hard life is at times, it can be unfair and cruel but also completely unavoidable. As the saying goes, 'always be kind as everyone you meet is fighting a battle which you know nothing about'. Those words are so true. I wish everyone could see their own worth and know they are good enough to accept circumstances and things which are good for them. Always remember that every decision we make has a domino effect onto other people's lives too, so please make your choices wisely. Everyone deserves happiness in their life's and to spend their short time in this world with people who will love and support them unconditionally. We only get one chance at life, don't waste it. Sadly there are also always people out there who seem to enjoy making life harder than it needs to be. Some people seem to love creating problems or dramas when it is really unnecessary and very easily avoided, I don't understand how anyone can get pleasure from making another person's life hard, it just doesn't make any sense to me.

The hurt from my past will always be there, I can never escape the memories, but I feel because I experienced so much at such a young age, I developed a way of handling it fairly well considering all of the unfortunate circumstances. With every positive experience I had, I immersed myself in those feeling's it brought with it. I could wipe away any negative feelings and live fully in those present moments. I don't dwell on my past and don't blame my past for anything, I simply recognise that if different situations had occurred, ultimately things would have been different. I accept full responsibility for my own life because holding on to negativity is only going to hurt me more and, more than likely, my children too. I realised this was the case a long time ago, and I'm so glad I did, because I didn't want negativity passed through me to them. My children are the product of a fresh start, they are cycle break children.

If you're feeling upset about something someone else did to you a very long time ago, are those feelings hurting the person who did it to you? No, I am sorry to say this, but I very much doubt they are. The only person your thoughts are hurting is you, the sooner that is realised the quicker you will learn to let any hurt from the past go.

It is a sad reality that people can hurt you and not know or even care about the long-term damage they are causing, one thing can often have a snowball effect and begin to cause more negative circumstances. I can guess that those who hurt you are probably getting on with their life without a thought for the harm they have caused you, living their life as if nothing has ever happened.

I vowed that I would treat my own children differently and I really do. I couldn't imagine inflicting any form of pain on to my beautiful children. I can't understand any reason for the way I was treated or how nothing was thought of it. But I know how it felt to be the one receiving such abuse. I know I would never want anyone to feel what I had felt over the years. To experience the worst pain of them all by having to bury my own child, which was out of anyone's control, is why I say that life is hard enough, without being surrounded by people who make life harder for the absolute fun of it.

I hope that my own children go on to grow up to be healthy, happy and well-balanced adults and the changes I have made ensure that they will live happy family lives, for generations to come. There is no one in the world more important than my own children.

If things are difficult for you at the moment, know it's not selfish to self-care. In fact it's the best thing you can do, because your family's happiness ultimately depends on your own happiness. If you're reading this from another perspective where you have never known this type of life, I am so happy and thankful you are happy and I hope this brings you an insight so you may be able to show compassion and understanding where it is truly needed.

Between 2018-2019 in the UK alone, 4.2 million children were living in poverty, this number is sadly always increasing. To know this very sad statistic, you will also know that these families are not only dealing with living in poverty, but they are also likely to be dealing with other problems too. Mental health issues, alcoholism, drug abuse, difficult living conditions, just to name a few. It breaks my heart to think that there are children everywhere living in less desirable circumstances. Children don't really crave the material things in life, you could be living right on the breadline, but your children will feel richer than anyone just by giving them your love and protecting them from any unnecessary pain. It's a fact of life that pain will one day come to us all. Let the children be children and flourish into the people they are meant to be. That was all I wanted when I was growing up, to love and to be loved. It was during the fleeting moments where I felt love which made me feel the happiest of all.

The more positives you can find in your life and the more grateful you are for those positive things, the happier you will become. A positive mindset will equal a positive mind. One small positive thought in the morning can change your entire day. If you can't think of much to be grateful for, look around you. Be grateful for waking up each day, the air that you breathe and the home which you live in. If you're lucky enough to be surrounded by family and friends, be grateful for them all. These were some of the techniques I learnt from reading Love Life, Live Life. I highly recommend grabbing yourself a copy.

I am so incredibly grateful that I have the most beautiful children, they bring so much joy into my life, they are always keeping me very busy. I am ridiculously grateful for my husband, he can brighten anyone's day who he meets. I am so thankful for my in-laws, for they are a constant support to myself and husband whilst also being the best grandparents to our children. I am thankful for my car and our beautiful home, also I am grateful for my dog who never leaves my side. I'm grateful for my health and my family's health. I'm also grateful for my bad experiences, for without them I wouldn't be the person I am today. I would like to say to them, "thank you for all the pain you caused me, for if I hadn't felt that pain I wouldn't have wished so much better for my own children, I would never have dreamed so big and ultimately they would not be living the good life they now have without you, so thank you". I'm truly grateful that, although I suffered, I am completely aware of what mistreatment feels like and therefore would never intentionally inflict pain onto anyone else, so thank you once again. With that, I've let it go, it can all stay in the past, I'm living in the present and I am so excited for what the future may bring.

I really hope my story has inspired you in some way and that you always remember who you truly are. Know that you are most certainly deserving, and you should also know by now that YOU are good enough. You definitely don't need fixing, and no one needs to fix you. All that you need to do is take responsibility for your own life, no one, but you can do that for you. Happiness comes from within yourself so please just do whatever it is that makes you happy and your happiness will surely follow. Start by focusing on what you want, and all that you don't want will fall away. Break free from negative hereditary patterns. No more regrets, ever.

Lots of love

Marley

Milton Keynes UK
Ingram Content Group UK Ltd.
UKHW020611010823
426133UK00011B/336